Outdoor Projects

Time-Life Books is a division of Time Life Inc.
Time-Life is a trademark of Time Warner Inc. and affiliated companies.

TIME LIFE INC.
CHAIRMAN AND CHIEF EXECUTIVE OFFICER: Jim Nelson
PRESIDENT AND CHIEF OPERATING OFFICER: Steven Janas
SENIOR EXECUTIVE VICE PRESIDENT AND CHIEF OPERATIONS OFFICER: Mary Davis Holt
SENIOR VICE PRESIDENT AND CHIEF FINANCIAL OFFICER: Christopher Hearing

TIME-LIFE BOOKS
PRESIDENT: Larry Jellen
SENIOR VICE PRESIDENT, NEW MARKETS: Bridget Boel
VICE PRESIDENT, HOME AND HEARTH MARKETS: Nicholas M. DiMarco
VICE PRESIDENT, CONTENT DEVELOPMENT: Jennifer L. Pearce

TIME-LIFE TRADE PUBLISHING
VICE PRESIDENT AND PUBLISHER: Neil S. Levin
SENIOR SALES DIRECTOR: Richard J. Vreeland
DIRECTOR, MARKETING AND PUBLICITY: Inger Forland
DIRECTOR OF TRADE SALES: Dana Hobson
DIRECTOR OF CUSTOM PUBLISHING: John Lalor
DIRECTOR OF RIGHTS AND LICENSING: Olga Vezeris

OUTDOOR PROJECTS
DIRECTOR OF NEW PRODUCT DEVELOPMENT: Carolyn M. Clark
NEW PRODUCT DEVELOPMENT MANAGER: Lori A. Woehrle
EXECUTIVE EDITOR: Linda Bellamy
DIRECTOR OF DESIGN: Kate L. McConnell
TECHNICAL SPECIALIST: Monika Lynde
DIRECTOR OF PRODUCTION: Carolyn Bounds
QUALITY ASSURANCE: Jim King and Stacy L. Eddy

Produced by Lark Books (a division of Sterling Publishing Co. Inc.), Asheville, North Carolina.
ART DIRECTOR: Thom Gaines
WOODWORKING EDITOR: Andy Rae
WILDLIFE AND FURNITURE EDITOR: Marcianne Miller
PRINCIPAL PHOTOGRAPHERS: Richard Hasselberg, Thom Gaines, Evan Bracken
ILLUSTRATOR: Orrin Lundgren
WATERCOLORIST: Lorraine Plaxico
EDITORIAL ASSISTANCE: Heather Smith, Emma Laurel Jones, Roper Cleland
RESEARCH ASSISTANCE: Holly Cowart, Carey Burda, Kendrick Weeks
TECHNICAL CONSULTANTS: Bo Harper (Bo Scapes Personal Gardening Service, Pickens, S.C.),
    Matt Fuscoe (Scott R. Melrose & Associates, P.A., Asheville, N.C.)

© 2001 Time-Life Inc

All rights reserved. No part of this book may be reproduced in any form or by any electronic or mechanical means, including information storage and retrieval devices or systems, without prior written permission from the publisher, except that brief passages may be quoted for reviews.

Printed in China.
10 9 8 7 6 5 4 3 2

School and library distribution by Time-Life Education, P.O. Box 85026, Richmond, Virginia 23285-5026.

ISBN 0-7370-0633-1

CIP data available upon application:
Librarian, Time-Life Books
2000 Duke Street
Alexandria, VA 22314

For information on and a full description of any of the Time-Life Books series, please call 1-800-621-7026 or write:

Reader Information
Time-Life Customer Service
P.O. Box C-32068
Richmond, Virginia 23261-2068

Outdoor Projects

CINDY BURDA

Contents

6	Introduction
8	**GARDEN PATHS AND WALKWAYS**
10	Choosing the Right Path
12	Path Materials
20	Preparing a Base for Your Path
27	Edging
28	Finishing Your Path: Adding the Surface Material
42	**GARDEN BORDERS**
44	Choosing a Border
46	Where to Put Your Border
48	Hedges
50	Planting a Hedge
52	Fences
58	Building a Picket Fence
60	Walls
64	Building a Mortared Stone Wall
66	Gates and Entryways
68	Enhancing Existing Borders
70	**GARDEN WILDLIFE**
72	Domestic Harmony
74	Attracting (and Deterring) Wildlife
78	Building a Bat House
80	Inviting Birds
83	Decorating a Purchased Birdbath with Mosaic

85	Inviting Butterflies
86	A Butterfly Garden Plan
88	Building a Butterfly Box

90 GARDEN FURNITURE

92	Selecting Outdoor Furniture
96	Buying Garden Furniture
97	Building Wooden Garden Furniture
98	Building a Portable Deck
100	Building an Adirondack Love Seat
104	Building an Outdoor Table & Matching Chair

110 APPENDIXES

110	Appendix A: When to Bring in the Professionals
110	Appendix B: More About Stone
113	Appendix B.1: Characteristics of Common Stone
113	Appendix C: More About Brick
114	Appendix C.1: Types of Brick
115	Appendix D: More About Woodworking for Outdoor Use
117	Appendix D.1: Properties of Common Wood for Outdoor Use
118	Appendix E: Softwood Lumber Sizes
118	Appendix F: Metric Conversions
119	Appendix G: USDA Hardiness - Zone Map
120	Acknowledgements
122	Bibliography
124	Index

Introduction

Few things reveal pride in home as clearly as a well-tended lawn and garden. And without a doubt, a lush stretch of grass and beds of flowers and vegetables can be among the true joys of home ownership. But if you take a look at a pristine lawn or a picture-perfect garden, you may notice something: Unless you're mowing or weeding or otherwise working, there doesn't seem to be a place for you—a place where you simply want to be.

This book is about creating that place, step by step, and project by project.

Start by making your lawn and garden more accessible—and inviting—with a garden path or walkway. Not only will you add function—a stable avenue for your wheelbarrow, or a dew-free route from back door to garden shed for yourself—you'll also add charm and beauty. Whether you want a simple trail of pine needles or a stately brick walkway, you'll find directions for creating it in the first chapter.

Then, shape and transform your outdoor space with a garden border. Hedges, fences, and walls can create privacy, filter gusty winds, offer security, or simply beautify your home. Explore what function(s) you want your border to fulfill, and learn which type will suit your needs best. Then plant a hedge, build a fence, or construct a wall—you'll find complete instructions for each in the second chapter.

Next, invite wildlife to share your space—birds, butterflies, bats, and others will make your garden and backyard a much more interesting and beautiful place to be. Read about which creatures to invite—and which to discourage—and learn how to do both. Build a bat house and a butterfly box. Decorate a purchased birdbath, and plant a butterfly garden. You'll enjoy the projects in the third chapter as much as your wild guests will.

Finally, give yourself and your family a place to relax by furnishing your outdoor space. The fourth chapter will help you choose the best garden furniture for your needs based on how you plan to use it, where you want to place it, and how much time you want to spend maintaining it. Read tips for buying and for building outdoor furniture. Then make a few projects, including a no-fuss patio, a great-looking outdoor table and matching chair, and a cozy Adirondack love seat.

If you need a little more information about stone, brick, or wood for outdoor use, turn to the appendix section at the back of the book. There, you'll find everything you need to know to select weather-resistant wood or the best brick for your project, as well as instructions for cutting brick, trimming stone, and even tips for deciding when to call in the professionals.

As you'll see in the pages that follow, transforming your outdoor space into the perfect place for you and your family is well within your reach. The possibilities are endless—and they're right in your own backyard!

Garden Paths & Walkways

Many people despair of ever finding the right path in life, be it to love, a fulfilling career, or spiritual enlightenment. Fortunately, selecting and creating the right path for your garden or backyard requires much less soul-searching! Whether you long to meander along a winding path through your rose garden, or just need to sprint from front door to car on a busy morning, this chapter will guide your way.

Start by clarifying why you want a path, where it will lead, and who will travel it. Then, based on your site and the kind of path you want, select the material. Compare cost and ease (or difficulty) of installation, and find out where to buy each type of material and how to calculate the amount you'll need for your path.

Next, learn how to check your path site's drainage and slope, and how to adjust each, if necessary. Excavate a base, choosing either a flexible gravel base or a more rigid concrete base. Finish your path by laying the surface material; you'll read about the best way to work with each kind, and you'll find tips for maintaining your path when it's complete.

After reading this chapter, you can be certain of choosing the right path—in one area of your life, anyway!

Choosing the Right Path

To choose the right path, start by asking yourself a few questions: Where will your path lead and who will walk it? Will it wind around a berm? Or will it lead directly to your front door? What is the climate like in your area? And the terrain? Finally, consider how much time and money you're willing to invest in creating your path. The answers will help you decide everything from whether to pave with grass or gravel, to how many (if any) twists and turns your trail will take.

WHERE WILL YOUR PATH LEAD AND WHO WILL WALK IT?

If you'd like to mark a route from driveway to front entry, your path should be direct, wide, and inviting.

A course through flower gardens should take a different direction. It should meander and curve and invite sauntering, rather than sprinting. Organic materials, such as bark mulch or crushed shells, lend a certain natural harmony to a garden. Pine needles offer the added enticement of their sun-warmed fragrance, and grass contrasts nicely with mulched flower beds.

Soft grass makes an inviting path to a seldom-visited secret alcove, but avoid it if you think your path will see heavy traffic; grass just won't hold up under frequent footsteps. Gravel, on the other hand, is attractive and durable, but not appropriate for paths likely to be trod by bare feet.

SITE CONSIDERATIONS

If you plan to build your path along your house or beside a shed, check the site's slope first (see pages 21 and 22). Water will need to be directed away from the building's foundation, so you may need to adjust the slope (see page 22). Choose a path material and style that match or complement the buildings your path will abut. Haphazardly placed, homemade mosaic stepping stones would make a charming trail through an informal garden; however, they may not be as suitable for the main walkway leading to a Gregorian mansion.

Pay attention to natural features, too. The roots of today's modest oak tree might expand five years down the road and buckle your well-laid brick path.

Deep freezes and ice can be just as damaging to inflexible paving materials as tree roots, so if you live in a part of the country that experiences harsh win-

A path of cut stone makes a direct and inviting entryway.

CHOOSING THE RIGHT PATH 11

ters, you may want to avoid concrete and brick. A grass path will grow beautifully in a sunny spot with plenty of rain, but a path of cut stone will probably just grow slippery in an area with too much moisture.

The terrain your path will cover will also help determine the material you choose. Gravel will stay put on slopes, while mulch or straw will be more likely to wash away in a heavy rain. Stone, cut or natural, is difficult to lay on rolling stretches, so opt for more flexible materials instead.

YOUR INVESTMENT

Building a path can be a weekend project, or it can be a major undertaking. The style, length, and paving material you choose will all determine which yours ends up being. An elaborate concert walkway will require a lot more time (and money) than a simple path of straw. Consider the tools and materials you'll need, too. The following is a list of the basic ones you'll need: safety equipment, including heavy-duty gloves, safety glasses, and ear plugs; a hard iron rake; a wheel barrow; a hammer and saw; a broom; layout tools, including a string level, a 4-foot-long level, and a 50- or 100-foot measuring tape; marking materials, including pin flags, inverted marking paint, and mason's twine; digging tools, including a mattock, a square-bladed shovel, a round-nosed shovel, and a foot adz hoe; pruning shears or a pruning saw (for clearing brush and cutting tough roots); a tamping tool; and—if you're working with concrete— trowels, a float, a screed, and an edging tool. To lay some path materials, you may need additional tools and materials; the section on finishing your path (pages 28 through 41) lists the extra supplies, if any, necessary to lay each type of paving material.

Organic materials are perfect for winding garden paths.

If you really want the more time-consuming path, but feel that every hour of your weekend is already spoken for, consider hiring a professional (see page 110). You can always satisfy your need to "do it yourself" by laying a few stepping stones through your rose garden.

For more information about individual path materials, see pages 12 through 19.

Path Materials

Take a look around any home improvement store and you'll find a bewildering variety of path-paving materials. Which one is best for your path? The following section gives an overview of the most common materials to help you make the right choice.

ORGANIC MATERIALS

Pine needles, mulches, crushed shells (sea and nut), straw, and earth are among the least expensive and easiest-to-work-with materials you can choose to build a path. They offer a rustic look that complements all but the most formal of gardens. Organic materials also conform well to slight dips, rises, and curves in the landscape, so they can be used on most sites; they are, however, prone to erosion on slopes.

You will have to replenish an organic-material path periodically. Rain and wind will take their toll, and you'll probably end up tracking at least some of your path indoors. In wet climates, organic materials can turn boggy, and they tend to sprout weeds. And although earth is quite durable (if muddy in the rain), most other organic materials won't stand up well under heavy use.

Depending on where you live, you may be able to gather some organic materials yourself in the woods. Otherwise, check with building-supply stores, garden centers, sawmills, and local farms. Some bark and most mulches are available in bulk and sold in bales by the cubic yard. Bulk suppliers will generally deliver to your home for a fee, or load your truck for free at their site. For smaller projects, you may want to consider buying materials by the bag. Bagged material is usually sold by the cubic foot.

To calculate the volume of organic material you'll need, multiple the length of your path by its width. Then multiply by the depth to which you want to fill the path. If you're working in feet, your result will be in cubic feet. To convert to cubic yards, divide by 27.

PATH MATERIALS

GRAVEL, CRUSHED STONE, AND DECORATIVE PEBBLES

Gravel and crushed stone give garden paths a more formal appearance than organic materials, but at a similar low cost. Decorative stones, such as river pebbles and marble chips, are also very handsome, but slightly more expensive. Gravel and decorative stone are available in a variety of colors, depending on where you live. (The gravel you buy will almost certainly have been quarried locally.)

Although not quite as simple as working with organic materials, mineral fill is fairly easy to build with. When properly graded, gravel paths drain quickly, hold well on moderate slopes, and conform to contours in the landscape. They're also durable and will retain their shape through winter freezes, spring melts, and assaults by expanding tree roots.

Gravel and other loose rock fills tend to migrate beyond path boundaries (particularly on steeply sloping sites), so you'll need to rake them back into place and replenish them from time to time. They're also prone to invasion by weeds, and the sharp edges of crushed stone can be hard on bare feet. Gravel larger than about ¾ inch is difficult to walk on, so stick to stone that's ⅜ inch or less.

Your local garden center or building supply store will carry gravel and decorative stone by the bag. Check the bags for volume as well as for weight. A 50-pound bag of pea gravel will cover fewer cubic feet than a 50-pound bag of volcanic rock because the former is denser than the latter. For larger projects, check with sand and gravel suppliers who sell by the cubic yard or the ton. If you live near a quarry, call to see if they sell to individuals. Some bulk suppliers will deliver for a fee, but most prefer that you come pick up gravel and stone yourself. Although it may not be as convenient, buying in bulk is less expensive than purchasing by the bag.

To determine how much loose rock fill you'll need for your path, multiply the path's length by its width and desired depth.

GRASS

The lush green of well-tended grass is a handsome partner for flower beds, herbaceous borders, and shrub gardens. With a little planning and (in some cases) a lot of watering, a grass path will grow in most parts of the country. The chart on the following page provides information to help you select the right grass for your climate. Consult with your local agricultural extension office and an area feed and seed store, too.

Depending on where it's located and how it's landscaped, a grass path can be a formal promenade or a casual walkway. In either case, it will always be cool and soft under bare feet. Grass will traverse and conform to slopes and even help prevent erosion. Laying sod is hard work, but sowing seeds falls into the moderate-effort category. You can sow a grass path from seed for just pennies per square foot. Sod strips, though much more costly than seed, are also reasonably inexpensive.

Of course, the money you save by sowing or installing a grass path may be spent later trying to keep it green, particularly if you live in a dry or drought-prone climate. If you start your path from seed, you'll need to stay off of it for several weeks while it sprouts. On sloped sites, erosion can be a problem during this early phase of growth, too. And, in general, grass won't hold up well to heavy traffic; it will, however, host plenty of weeds. Finally, if you don't enjoy mowing your lawn, you won't like mowing your path any better!

You can buy grass seed at any home and garden center or hardware store. Up until a few years ago, you could purchase it loose; today, however, most places only sell prebagged grass seed. Your salesperson will be able to help you determine how much you'll need for the area you want to cover. Price will vary from year to year and according to variety.

Although you can purchase sod strips at many garden centers, you'll get a better deal (and fresher sod) if you buy directly from a sod farm. Sod is usually priced by the square yard. To determine how much you'll need, just multiply the length of your path by its width. Then call ahead so it can be cut and ready when you get there. If you have a minimum order and don't mind paying a fee, most sod companies will deliver.

CUT STONE

Usually square or rectangular, uniform slabs of cut stone are ideal for creating formal, stately paths. Laid properly, cut stone can provide a smooth, handsome walkway, perfect for a main entry. You can mortar cut stone in place, dry-lay it in a bed of sand or gravel, or arrange it in a simple stepping-stone pattern (see page 33). In the first two arrangements, a cut-stone path is essentially permanent.

Which is fortunate, because laying one can be a hard, somewhat expensive job that you won't want to do often! Avoid using cut stone for sloping walkways or ramps; their flat surfaces gets slick when wet, and downright dangerous in icy conditions. The ice isn't just dangerous for

Common Grasses

TYPE OF GRASS	HARDINESS ZONE	SUN REQUIREMENTS	WATER NEEDS	DURABILITY
Bahia grass	9–10	*Grows well in sun or shade*	HIGHLY DROUGHT RESISTANT	Excellent durability
Beach grass	5–11, in sandy regions	*Full sun to moderate shade*	DROUGHT RESISTANT	Medium durability
Bent grass	8, in very humid regions	*Can stand 50-60% shade with good air and drainage*	WATERING USUALLY NECESSARY	Light durability
Bermuda grass	7–8, in cool, humid regions	*Full Sun*	REQUIRES IRRIGATION IN DRYER REGIONS	Excellent durability
Carpet grass	8–10, in warm, moist regions	*Tolerates moderate shade*	REQUIRES FREQUENT WATERING IN DRY AREAS	Light durability
Centipede grass	8, in warm regions	*Likes full sun best, can tolerate slight shade*	DROUGHT TOLERANT	Good durability
Fescue	3–6 and 8, in cool regions	*Highly tolerant of shade*	GOOD DROUGHT RESISTANCE	Medium durability
Kentucky bluegrass	3–6	*Will tolerate medium shade*	DROUGHT RESISTANT	Good durability
Rye grass	8, in cool regions	*Prefers sun, but will tolerate mild shade*	NEEDS TO REMAIN MOIST	Excellent durability
Zoysia	7, in warm regions	*Slightly shade tolerant*	DROUGHT RESISTANT	Excellent durability

you, either; extreme cold can crack and split this pricey material.

You can buy cut stone from masonry suppliers, stone yards, and tile companies. If you own or can borrow a pickup truck, you can haul your purchase yourself. Otherwise, most suppliers charge a flat fee to deliver locally, and some add a mileage charge, too. Cut stone is sold by the square foot or meter, and the price will vary according to the size of the slabs and the type and color of the stone. Depending on where you live, you may have access to limestone, sandstone, bluestone, slate, basalt, gneiss, or granite. (See the chart on page 113 for more information about each of these types of stone.)

The quantity of cut stone you'll need will depend on your path design; however, the salesperson at your supplier will be able to help you estimate the necessary amount, given the total surface area you plan to cover: Just multiply the length of your path times its width.

NATURAL STONE: FIELDSTONE AND FLAGSTONE

Fieldstone, as its name implies, is collected from fields or from old stone walls. Flagstone is quarried from large rock masses. Both come in various colors, shapes, and sizes, but stones with at least one very flat surface are best for path building. Fieldstone tends to be rougher and more weathered than flagstone, which usually has a cleaner, jagged look. Depending on how they're used, fieldstone and flagstone can achieve a number of different effects. Spaced haphazardly in green grass or interspersed with plantings, natural stone has a charming rustic quality. Fitted together like a jigsaw puzzle and laid in a mortar base, it can look as formal as a path from cut stone. Natural stone is generally very durable, and it can be used on areas that have a slight slope. And because part of natural stone's appeal is its irregular shape, you can cut and trim it to fit a given area or pattern.

PATH MATERIALS

(See pages 111 and 112 for directions for cutting and trimming stone.)

The difficulty of working with natural stone will vary according to the type of path. Laying stones one after another in a simple stepping-stone style is much easier than fitting together a jigsaw puzzle of stones in a mortar base. And be careful with that mortar base! If mixed improperly, it will crumble in just a year or two. Dry-laid stones have their problems, too. They tend to heave in frost and cold weather. Winter weather can be hard on stone no matter how it's set; water that collects in its dips and crevices will turn to ice—slippery for you, and damaging for your path.

You may be able to buy flagstone at your local quarry, although most deal in much larger quantities than what you'll need for a path. And no matter how big your truck or car is, parking it next to the enormous equipment at a quarry can be intimidating! A stone yard might be a better bet, and they often carry fieldstone as well as flagstone. Prices will vary dramatically, depending on the thickness, size, color, and type of stone. The best stones for path building are large, flat, and between 3 and 4 inches thick. Fieldstone will be more expensive than flagstone, and you'll pay more for both if you want to handpick them.

Natural stone is generally sold by the ton; however, your salesperson will be able to tell you about how much stone you'll need to cover a given area of square feet. To find the square feet, multiply the path's length by its width.

BRICK

Whether you want a formal front walkway or a homey path through the woods, you can make it with brick. Brick comes in so many colors, shapes, and styles and can be laid in so many different patterns that there's almost no limit to the kind of path you can build with it. Its standard size makes it easy to lay and to quantify. It also looks great in combination with other materials—as the edging for a gravel path or seguing into cut stone, for instance. New brick, in a well-laid path, is very durable. Older brick, although very charming, may not hold up as well.

Brick, old or new, will eventually buckle if it's laid over or near growing tree roots. It's also subject to cracking

18 GARDEN PATHS & WALKWAYS

and crumbling in very cold weather, and will grow mossy and slick in rainy climates. Planning and laying a brick path takes time and strict attention to detail, particularly for intricate patterns. And if you ever need to replace bricks or add to an existing path, you might have a hard time matching brick colors.

Brick suppliers, tile companies, and home and building supply centers all stock brick. You can haul about 1,000 pounds of brick yourself in a full-size pickup truck; however, most suppliers will deliver for a fee. The cost of brick will vary depending on how many and what style you buy. Just be sure to buy paving bricks, rather than facing bricks; the latter are designed for building walls.

Typical brick pavers measure 2¼ inches thick, 3¼ inches wide, and 8 inches long. Five typical brick pavers will cover about 1 square foot. To figure out how many bricks you'll need, multiply the length of your path times its width. Just keep in mind that bricks do come in a variety of shapes and sizes, and that a brick laid on its edge will cover less area than a brick laid on its face.

CONCRETE

Concrete can be used to achieve almost any kind of effect. Lay a straight, smooth path, or one that winds and curves and dips over slopes. You can color concrete. Embed it with seashells, pebbles, brick, or tile. Texture it with a broom, leaves, or even your own handprints. Pour cement into molds to make your own concrete pavers, or buy pre-made concrete pavers—the latter can be used just like brick, but come in an even larger selection of colors, shapes, and styles. In short, with concrete, you can build whatever kind of path suits your fancy. Additionally, when mixed and poured correctly, concrete paths are quite durable, and they're easy to keep clean, too.

On the downside, poured concrete is the most labor-intensive of the path materials described in this chapter. (Pre-made concrete pavers are much easier to work with.) It can require special equipment and very careful planning. Like other rigid path materials, concrete tends to crack and crumble in cold climates, and growing

PATH MATERIALS 19

tree roots will cause it to heave and buckle. Concrete can get hot during the summer and icy during the winter. And, of course, it's hard to correct mistakes in this kind of path; once concrete has set, the only way to change it is to break it to pieces and start all over.

You have several options for how to buy the materials for a concrete path. All home and building supply centers carry premixed concrete by the bag; this is Portland cement (the raw material for concrete) blended with the correct ratio of sand and gravel. All you do is add water per the instructions on the bag. It's widely available in 60- and 80-pound bags. You can also buy Portland cement, usually available in 94-pound bags, at home and building supply centers; you'll need to add sand and gravel (or another aggregate), as well as water, and mix the resulting cement in a wheelbarrow or in a power cement mixer. Finally, you can order ready-to-pour concrete by the cubic yard; a truck will come right to your home and pour exactly where you specify.

Bagged, premixed concrete is the most expensive option, but also the most convenient. Mixing your own concrete from cement, gravel, and sand costs about half as much, but involves a lot more hassle (plus, for larger jobs, the rental of a cement mixer). The cost of having ready-to-pour concrete delivered to your home hovers about midway between the first two options; however, you must be ready to work as soon as the material is poured, and you can't stop until the job is done. Ready-to-pour is appropriate for large jobs where several people are available to pitch in and help.

To determine how much concrete you'll need, multiply the length of your path by its width. Then multiply that figure by the path's depth. If you're working in feet, the result will be in cubic feet. Divide by 27 to convert to cubic yards. A bag of premixed concrete or Portland cement will generally say how much coverage it provides.

GARDEN PATHS & WALKWAYS

Preparing a Base for Your Path

Gravel or mulch, concrete or brick, all well-laid paths have one thing in common: a good base beneath. Even a grass path requires one, although you may not think of it as a base at all. (See page 31.) For most other types of paths, you should lay either a flexible base of gravel or a rigid base of concrete. The chart on page 24 offers general guidelines for which kind of base works best for each of the path materials described in this book. The following pages will walk you through the steps of building both types.

But before you excavate even an inch of earth, test your soil's drainage, lay out and mark the course of your path, and measure and (if necessary) adjust the slope along the path site.

DRAINAGE
A path that drains poorly is a path that won't stay in place very long. Fortunately, you can amend most drainage problems. To determine what steps, if any, you'll need to take, start by examining the type of soil at your site. Sandy or gravelly soil usually drains well. Clay and heavy topsoil tend to retain water, so additional water will sheet off of them, possibly damaging surrounding vegetation. Loam is a cross between sandy and clay soils, and drains accordingly.

To test your soil's drainage, dig an approximately 12-inch-deep, 4-inch-diameter hole somewhere along the path site. Fill the hole with water and let it drain. Then fill it again. If it takes more than 12 hours to drain the second time, your site has poor drainage. To improve drainage, dig your base at the deepest level suggested for the base and path type you're building. If you're building a gravel base, you may also want to add a drainage pipe, a process described on pages 25 and 26.

LAYING OUT YOUR PATH
Next, lay out where your path will be. Start by determining its width, allowing 2 feet per person, or 4 feet for a person in a wheelchair. Allow another foot for lawn-care equipment. So if you'd like your path to accommodate

Clay, loam, and sandy soil

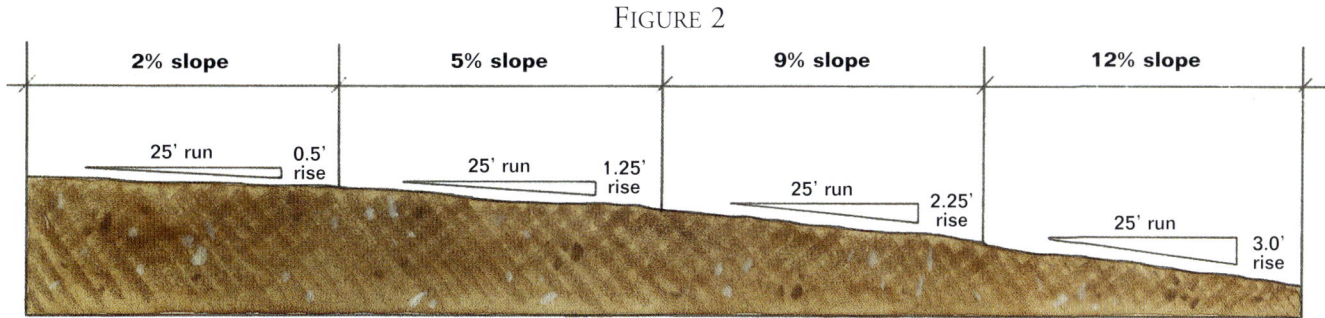

FIGURE 2

Slope is calculated by dividing the change in elevation, or "rise," by the distance traveled, or "run."

one person and a wheelbarrow, it will need to be at least 3 feet wide; to accommodate two people walking side by side, or one person in a wheelchair, your path should be at least 4 feet wide. Some edging materials (see page 27) require a small "shelf" hollowed out in the path base, too, so if you're using one of these materials, allow for the extra inches at this stage.

Define the path's borders by placing pin flags or stakes at intervals of about 6 feet. If the path will curve and wind, mark it with garden hoses or rope first; then mark the borders with pin flags or stakes before removing the hoses or rope. Be careful to maintain a consistent width along the path's entire route. When you're happy with the layout, spray the borders with inverted marking paint. If you'd like to add steps, mark the areas where you want them, too.

DEGREES OF SLOPE

The incline, or slope, at your site will affect drainage, the comfort of those traveling it, and the potential migration of path materials. If your site is too flat—with an incline of 1½ percent or less—you'll need to grade it across its width (a practice known as cross-slope grading). Otherwise, water will collect and stand in your path. An incline this slight, however, will be comfortable for walkers, and stable for any kind of path material.

A gentle slope—between 1½ and 3 percent—makes for prime walking; most people won't even notice the slight incline. Slopes between 5 and 8 percent are still considered gentle; however, at the steeper end of this range, some of the lighter organic materials may tend to wash slightly in heavy rains.

You can take advantage of a gentle slope to direct water off and away from your path, or to carry water along the path's run toward an existing drainage area. To check the natural drainage pattern, go outside during a heavy storm and simply watch where the water flows. If you'd prefer to stay dry, sprinkle the area with pine bark chips or some other material that floats. After the next heavy rain, note where the material ends up; it will show the site's natural run-off pattern.

Steeper sites—those with slopes of between 8 and 10 percent—will also drain well. If you decide to build a path on a site that slopes more than 10 percent, consider adding steps or cutting the path across the slope to make it easier to travel. (The sidebar on page 26 describes one method of adding steps to a steep path.) If your path runs up and down the slope on a site this steep, loose materials such as gravel and mulch will wash away, and your path will be extremely slippery when it's icy.

DETERMINING SLOPE

Just as in geometry, the slope of a path site is calculated with the formula "rise over run." That is, you divide the change in the altitude of the ground (the rise) by the distance traveled over the ground (the run). For instance, if the ground drops 1 inch for every 12 inches traveled, the slope would be 1 inch divided by 12 inches, or 8.3

percent. Your house site is probably already graded to direct water away from the foundation of your home; the standard slope is about 2 percent, or ¼ inch per foot. Figure 2 on the previous page shows several degrees of slope, based on a 25-foot run.

The best way to find the overall slope of your path site is with a string level. As its name implies, this is a level suspended on a string. To use it, start by pounding two stakes into the ground: one at your planned path's highest point, and one at the lowest point. Pulling the string taut, tie one end to each stake. Adjust the string until the level's air bubble rests in the center of the vial, indicating that the string is even. (See figure 3.) Enlist someone to help so that one person can check the bubble while the other person adjusts the string. When the string is level, measure the distance from the string to the ground at each stake. Take the difference between each end and divide that figure by the length of your path (or the section of your path you're working with). For instance, say your path is 50 feet long and the distance from the string to the ground is 1 foot at one end and 2 feet at the other end. The difference is 1 foot, so divide that by the length of the path, 50 feet. The result is .02, or 2 percent. Congratulations! Your site's slope is ideal for a path!

ADJUSTING SLOPE

Chances are, though, that your site may need some adjusting. Start by clearing the area of any tree stumps, concrete, or sod. If you plan to pave with a rigid material, make sure the ground is fairly smooth, too.

To actually adjust the slope, you'll probably need to move some earth—either by adding dirt to areas that are too low, or by removing dirt from areas that are too high. If your path is less than about 30 feet long and 3 feet wide, hand tools and some muscle should be sufficient for the job: Loosen the soil with a mattock; then use a square-bladed shovel to skim soil off high areas. Move it to low areas with a wheelbarrow, and add the soil in 6-inch layers, compacting each layer with a hand-held tamper as you go. For longer and wider paths, consider renting a front-end loader for the afternoon.

As you grade your site, use a level with double lines on the vial to monitor your progress; a 4-foot-long model is best for path-building. Start by placing the level on a flat, even surface. Then raise one end to the slope position you want for your site. For instance, if you want a 2-percent slope, lift one end of your 4-foot-long level 1 inch. (You'd lift a 2-foot-long level 1/2 inch for a 2-percent slope.) Note where the vial's bubble rests; then, each time you reach a change of slope along your path, check the site against that position, and add or remove dirt as necessary.

DIGGING THE BASE

The standard depth for a flexible gravel path base is between 6 and 7 inches, and about 8 inches for a rigid concrete base. However, the proper depth for your base will vary depending on the climate in your area and on

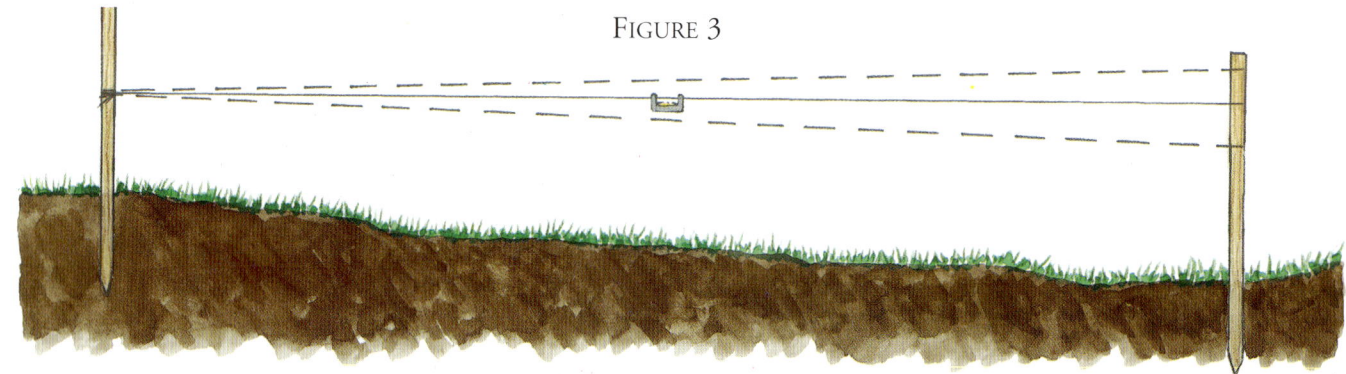

FIGURE 3

PREPARING A BASE FOR YOUR PATH

the type of paving material you're using. The chart on the following page lists appropriate base depths for common path materials. Contact a local landscape architect if you live in a climate that's subject to hard freezes or heavy rains; (s)he will be able to tell you how deep your base needs to be in order to make your path less vulnerable to seasonal heaving.

Dig out your base. If you're using edging that requires a shelf (see page 27), excavate the shelves now, too. If you're pouring a concrete base, remove 4 to 6 inches of additional earth on each side of the bed, about 4 inches deep; you'll use this extra space to set form boards (see page 25). With a mattock or a foot adz hoe, loosen and carve out packed earth, remove embedded rocks, and cut out small roots. Use a shovel to place the loosened earth into a wheelbarrow and to smooth the sides and bottom of the base. As you work, check the slope of your base with a level.

ADDING MATERIALS FOR A GRAVEL BASE

Fill your path base with a 4-inch layer of washed gravel. If your site has very good drainage and you'd like more stability, consider using "crusher run" gravel (sometimes called "road bond"), instead; this mixture of crushed stone and rock dust compacts to an almost concrete-like fixed base, but retains enough flexibility to accommodate growing tree roots and other path-shifting forces.

Level the gravel or crusher run with a shovel. If you're cross-slope grading to improve drainage, rake or shovel the gravel for a 2-percent slope. Then, working from the lowest part of your path up, pack the gravel by walking back and forth across it. For larger jobs, you may want to rent a lawn roller.

Many professional landscapers add non-woven landscape cloth at this stage. This synthetic material will filter sediment from draining storm water and prevent weeds from sprouting in the middle of your path. It's available at garden centers in widths of 3, 4, and 6 feet. Buy a

Calculating the Amount of Sand and Gravel You'll Need

To determine how much sand and gravel you'll need for your path base, multiply the width of the path by its length, in feet. Then multiply that figure by the depth to which you're going to fill the base with gravel, also in feet. Perform the same calculation for sand. This will give you the amount of each material in cubic feet. Divide by 27 to convert to cubic yards, the units in which most suppliers sell sand and gravel. Here's how:

Path length: 35 feet
Path width: 4 feet
Gravel depth: 3 inches or .25 feet

35 ft × 4 ft × .25 ft = 35 ft³
35 ft³ ÷ 27 = 1.3 cubic yards

WHAT IF I'M ADDING A DRAINPIPE?

As you'll see on pages 25 and 26, a drainpipe should sit in a gravel-filled, V-shaped trough the length and half the width of the path. To determine how much gravel you'll need to fill this trough, multiply the length of the path times half its width, in feet. Then multiply the result by the depth of the trough at the deepest part of the V, also in feet. Then, as above, convert this figure to cubic yards by dividing by 27. For example:

Path length: 35 feet
Path width: 4 feet
Gravel depth: 3 inches or .25 feet

35 ft × 2 ft × .25 ft = 17.5 ft³
17.5 ft³ ÷ 27 = .65 cubic yard

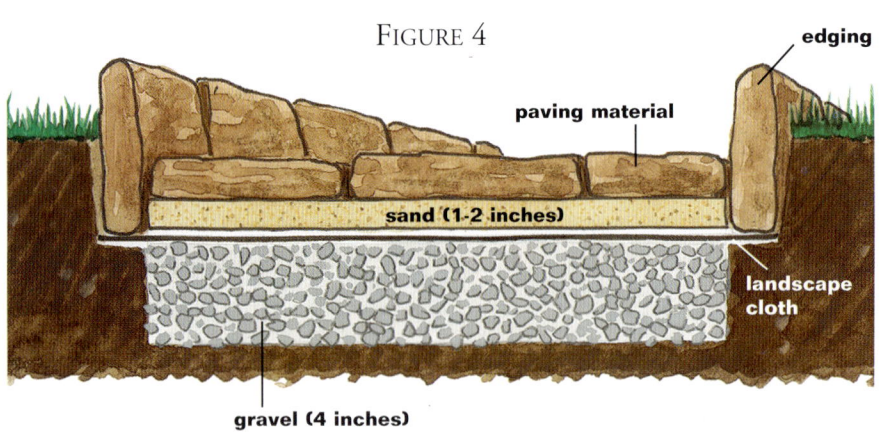

FIGURE 4

Base Depths for Common Path Materials

A gravel base works well for these path types:

PATH TYPE	BASE DEPTH
Organic material	6 inches
Gravel and ornamental stone	4 inches in well-draining soil, 7 inches in poorly draining soil
Stepping stones	See page 29
Dry-laid cut stone	6 to 7 inches
Dry-laid brick or concrete pavers	6 to 7 inches
Larger sizes of dry-laid natural stone	6 to 7 inches

A concrete base works well for these path types:

PATH TYPE	BASE DEPTH
Mortared cut stone	8 inches
Thin or brittle dry-laid cut stone	8 inches
Mortared natural stones	8 inches
Mortared brick or concrete pavers	8 inches
Smaller sizes of dry-laid natural stones	8 inches
Any other type of path for which a very stable, permanent base is desired	6 to 8 inches

width large enough to completely span your path. If you're using edging, you'll stack it on top of the cloth, so make sure there's enough material on both sides of the path to do this.

Smooth a 1-inch layer of sand over the landscape cloth (or over the gravel, if you didn't use landscape cloth.) Simply rake the sand into place and add your paving material. Figure 4 shows a cross section of a typical gravel base.

POURING CEMENT FOR A CONCRETE BASE

The soil in your path bed needs to be well compacted before you pour cement. A power tamper can drop the grade by an inch or more, so a hand tamping tool is the best choice for this job. If you need to grade for a cross slope, do that now, adding or removing dirt and compacting it wherever necessary. If your soil is firm and stable, you can move right on to placing form boards (see below).

If your path is on unstable soil, you'll need to reinforce the base by adding strength to the concrete. To do this, lay either wire mesh or rods of #4 steel rebar in the path base on top of chunks of rock or brick. Another option, if you're using ready-to-pour cement, is to order your cement from the supplier premixed with fiberglass.

Form boards placed along the sides of your path base will hold the cement in place as you pour it, establish a strong edge for your path, and allow you to monitor the slope of the cement. You can make form boards for the straight portions of your path from wooden stakes and scrap 2 x 4 or 2 x 6 lumber. For curved portions, use 4-inch-wide strips of particle board instead of 2x lumber. If your path is relatively flat, start by nailing the wooden stakes to what will be the outside face of the boards at intervals of 3 to 4 feet. Install the form boards by driving the stakes into the ground. On sloped sites, place the boards in the base first. Drive the stakes in behind; then, supporting the stakes from behind, nail the boards to them. Figure 5 shows a path base with form boards in place.

If you want your path to have a cross slope, you may need to adjust the form boards. Start by placing your level across the boards; or—if the path is too wide or your level is too short—place a scrap piece of 2x lumber across the form boards, and place the level on top of that. Raise or lower the form boards as necessary to achieve the desired slope.

If you're mixing your own cement, a good recipe for a path base is 1 part Portland cement, 2 parts clean river sand, and 3 parts gravel. You can also use premixed, bagged cement, or have ready-to-pour cement delivered to your site in a cement truck. If you're mixing your own or preparing bagged mix, consider renting a cement mixer for the day; otherwise, use a wheelbarrow and a hoe to mix it.

Pour 3 to 4 inches of cement into the base. Allow it to set at least overnight before laying the paving material. After the concrete has set, you can either tear out the form boards and reuse them, or leave them in place and cover them with dirt. If you're going to mortar your surface material in place, just follow the instructions given for the specific type of path material (see pages 28 through 41). If you'd like to dry-lay your paving material, allow the concrete base to set at least overnight; then finish it with a 1-inch layer of fine-grained sand, and follow the directions given for dry-laying the specific paving material. Figure 6 shows a cross section of a typical concrete base with a layer of sand.

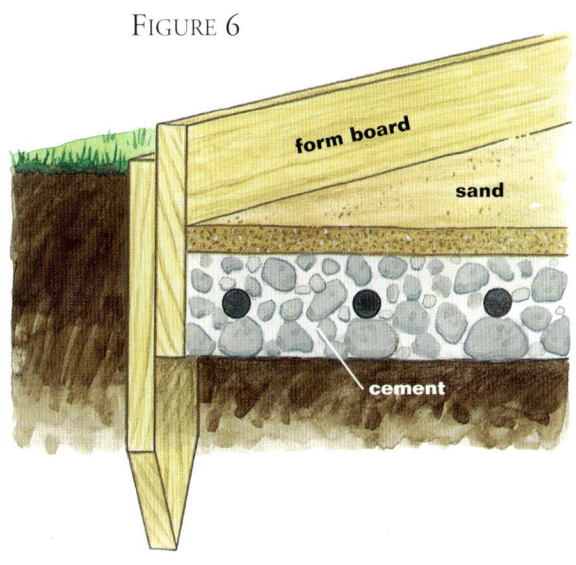

FIGURE 6

ADDING A DRAINPIPE

One of the best ways to improve your path's drainage is by placing a 4-inch-diameter (or larger) plastic drainpipe in the base along the entire length of the path. Instead of creating a base with a rectangular profile, dig a roughly triangular trough, with the deepest point at about 8 inches. Fill the trough with a 2-inch layer of

FIGURE 5

gravel. Some drainpipes come with a special sock to help keep sediment from seeping in. If yours didn't, wrap it in landscape cloth instead. Place the socked or wrapped drainpipe on top of the gravel; then cover it with 5 or 6 more inches of gravel. Lay the landscape cloth in place, as described on pages 23 and 24. Top the landscape cloth with a 1-inch layer of sand. Add your surface material so that it's just flush with the ground. (In most cases, the paving material should rise about 1 inch above the ground.) Figure 7 shows a cross section of a path with a drainpipe in the base.

Make sure the drainpipe doesn't empty at a place where the water might stand and collect—such as a flat spot at the bottom of your path. Either direct the runoff away from the bottom of the path, or grade the bottom of the path with a slight slope.

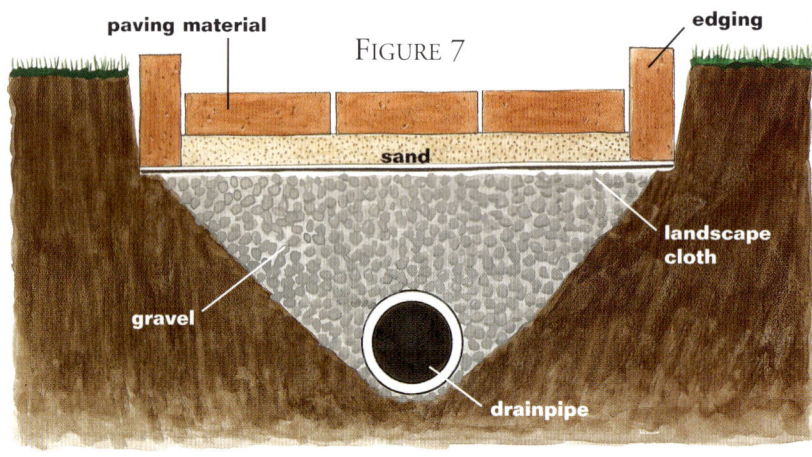

FIGURE 7

Adding Steps to a Steeply Sloping Site

If your path traverses a stretch with a grade in excess of 8 percent, you may want to add steps to it. One of the easiest ways to do this is with pressure-treated landscape timbers or short lengths of log. (If you use logs, be sure to treat them with a penetrating wood preservative first.) Start by clearing and marking the area where you want to add steps, just as you would for a regular path: Remove plants, leaves, and topsoil; then mark the borders with pin flags and inverted marking paint. Measure the height between where you want to top step and the bottom step. Then divide that measurement by the height of your steps (the width of the landscape timbers or logs); this will give you the number of steps you'll need.

Working from the bottom of the slope to the top, place the timbers or logs at even, easy-to-step intervals. Compact the soil behind each one as you go. Take a test walk to make sure the steps are spaced for comfortable climbing. Make adjustments, if necessary. Then drill two centered 3/8-inch holes through the top face of each step, locating the holes about 6 inches in from each end. Secure the steps by driving a 24-inch-long piece of #5 rebar through each hole. You can leave the earth between the steps bare, or excavate a shallow base at each step and add a layer gravel or bark mulch.

Edging

You may decide to forgo edging for informal paths. However, whether you choose simple fieldstone laid on top of the ground or handsome, partially buried landscape timbers, edging serves both practical and aesthetic functions. It will help keep your paving materials in and weeds and grass out. Most kinds of edging will also give your path added detail and style.

Edging set on top of the ground requires little more than placing the material in a pleasing pattern after you've completed the path surface. For added durability, however, start by digging a shelf in your path base, as described on page 23. For materials set in an area that needs mowing, excavate the shelf deep enough so that the top surface of your edging will be no more than ½ inch above the ground. If you're using landscape cloth, lay it first. Then set the edging on top of it. (See figure 8.)

A shelf with the proper dimensions will hold most edging materials firmly in place. Landscape timbers are the exception. To keep them in place, start by boring ⅝-inch-diameter holes at 3-foot intervals through the center of each timber. Position the timbers in the edging shelves; then use a sledge hammer to drive a 24-inch length of #5 rebar through each hole, into the ground below. The top of each piece of rebar should be flush with the top of the timber.

If you choose commercial plastic or vinyl edging, it will probably have loops attached at its base. To hold this kind of edging in place, just drive stakes through the holes.

COMMON EDGING MATERIALS

- Brick, in color(s) that match or complement your path
- Fieldstone
- Pre-formed plastic, aluminum, or vinyl edging
- Pressure-treated 2 x 4 or 2 x 6 lumber
- Pressure-treated landscape timbers
- Anything else that strikes your fancy, from seashells to ceramic tiles

FIGURE 8

Fieldstone edging

Pre-formed plastic edging

Finishing Your Path: Adding the Surface Material

Digging and preparing a base is the most labor-intensive part of building most paths. In fact, if you're using organic materials or gravel as the final paving material, the bulk of your work is already done. The next few pages cover the specifics of the final step in creating your path: laying the paving material.

ORGANIC MATERIALS

Finish the base for an organic-material path by adding a 2- to 4-inch layer of bark mulch over the landscape cloth and sand (or over the gravel, if you're not using a landscape cloth.) This will give your path a nice, springy foundation; it will also help prevent (or at least postpone) "bald spots"— areas where the path's surface material has eroded or worn thin and the landscape cloth shows through.

If you're using bark mulch as your surface material, simply add another 2-inch layer; then rake it for an even finish. For other organic materials, this final surface layer should be between 4 and 6 inches thick to allow for compaction.

Maintenance

Keep an eye on the surface layer; you may need to replenish it from time to time throughout the year.

GRAVEL AND ORNAMENTAL STONE

Before adding the final layer to a gravel or ornamental stone path, be sure to install edging of some kind (page 27). Otherwise, your gravel isn't likely to stay in place very long. The top surface of the path's base should be about 1 inch below ground level. Add enough gravel or ornamental stone to raise the path's surface until it's just even with, or slightly higher than, the surrounding ground. Smooth the gravel with a hard iron rake, water it well, then pack it with a tamper or a lawn roller.

FINISHING YOUR PATH

Maintenance

To keep your gravel path looking its best, rake it from time to time. If the path is on a slope, be sure to rake from the bottom up, since gravel tends to migrate downhill. Hoe or pull any weeds that sprout. Unless your path is very heavily traveled, you probably won't need to replenish the surface layer for several years.

STEPPING STONES

Additional Tools and Materials

- Garden trowel or straight-nosed spade
- Sand

Among the easiest to build, stepping-stone paths are also often the most charming and appealing. Natural stone is probably the most popular stepping "stone" choice, but you can also use concrete pavers, cut stone, or even wooden rounds you cut yourself from logs. (Just be sure to treat your rounds with a penetrating wood preservative before laying them; otherwise, they'll rot quickly when placed in the ground.) Figure 9 on the following page shows typical stepping stone path styles.

For a very stable path, lay your stepping stones on a flexible gravel base. Fill in around the stones with gravel, sand, or the soil you removed when you dug the base. In most cases, though, you can simply excavate a patch of earth to fit each stepping stone, and line it with an inch or two of sand. The patch should be deep enough to allow the set stone to sit flush with the surrounding ground.

Before you buy or set your "stones," though, take some time to design your path. Keep these tips in mind:

- Use similarly shaped and relatively large (but not huge) "stones."
- Plan to set stones no more than 4 to 5 inches apart. Your path will be able to accommodate many different walkers, and their varying strides, if the spaces between stones are easy to cross.
- Try to keep your path as straightforward as possible. A path that winds and twists and staggers back and forth may look interesting, but

it will probably also look (and, in fact, be) difficult to travel.

- In general, stepping stones should cross the path route lengthwise, not parallel to it.
- Start your path with larger stones to mark the threshold. Use larger stones at transitional points, too, to alert travelers to the change.
- Look for flat stones that won't collect water on their surfaces.
- Avoid slippery stones such as marble and slate.

Before excavating the base patches for each stone, lay out your path on the ground. Take a walk along it to make sure the layout will be comfortable to travel. Adjust it as necessary. When you're happy with the design, leave the stones in place. Cut the soil around each one, using a garden trowel or a flat-nosed spade. Move the stones aside and remove soil as necessary, keeping in mind that the set stones should sit flush with the ground. Line each patch with 1 to 2 inches of sand. Put the stones back in place. Use your hands to settle the stones into the sand; then give each one a few taps with a rubber mallet to set them.

Maintenance

You may need to reset stones occasionally. If your path runs through a grassy spot, such as your lawn, you'll probably have to trim around it with a weed-eater equipped with a string blade.

GRASS

Additional Tools and Materials
- Rototiller (optional)
- High-phosphate or super-phosphate fertilizer

For laying sod, you'll also need:
- Hatchet
- Rototiller (optional)
- Small piece of plywood for use as a kneeling board
- Sod staples (available at garden supply stores)
- Lawn roller
- Hose and sprinkler

For sowing seed, you'll also need:
- Rototiller (optional)
- Drop-seeder
- Lawn roller
- Hose and sprinkler
- Hay or straw for mulch

A grass path requires a slightly different approach than most other path types. For instance, you won't need to dig and prepare a gravel or concrete base. Instead, start by taking a soil sample from the area where you plan to lay your path. Send the sample to your local agricultural extension office; they can run tests on it and tell you how to treat your soil to produce the healthiest grass. They may also have suggestions for grass species that will grow well in your area and soil. Check the grasses chart on page 15 for other possibilities.

FIGURE 9

Cut stone

Concrete pavers

Natural stone

FINISHING YOUR PATH

Layout and mark the borders of your path as described on pages 20 and 21. Then clear the entire path area of rocks, roots, weeds, and unwanted grass. Cut out and remove the old grass with a flat-nosed shovel, a foot adz hoe, or—if you have a very large area to clear—a rented sod cutter. Then break up the earth with a mattock or a rototiller.

Treat the soil as recommended by your agricultural extension office. They might suggest adding lime to raise the pH level, or high-phosphate starter fertilizer to encourage growth. Rake the soil well so it's broken to a depth of at least 2 inches and any fertilizer is well blended. Your path "base" is now ready to be seeded or covered with sod strips.

Laying Sod

Pick up or have your sod delivered as close as possible to the time you plan to install it. Sod will keep for a few days in cool, wet weather; but under hot sun, it will yellow and start to die in just 12 hours.

Lightly water the path's soil. Then, if necessary, cut the sod into useable strips with a spade or a hatchet. Begin laying strips at one end of the path and work toward the other end. Make sure the edges fit together tightly so that the pieces don't dry out. Alternate the joints, too, as shown in figure 10.

If your path is on a steep incline, lay the strips lengthwise and cross-slope; this will help prevent erosion. Hold the uphill-side edges in place with heavy wire sod staples. (Remove the staples after two or three weeks, after the sod has rooted.) To avoid damaging the sod, kneel on a small piece of plywood as you work; otherwise, your knees will gouge into the fresh, somewhat fragile grass as you move from one area of the path to the next.

After you've laid the path, press it firmly into place with a lawn roller, being careful to even out any bumps. The sod's roots must get pressed into the soil, and if you leave any air pockets they can dry out. Fill any gaps between the sod strips with damp topsoil. (Grass will grow into these spots quickly.) Then water the entire path well.

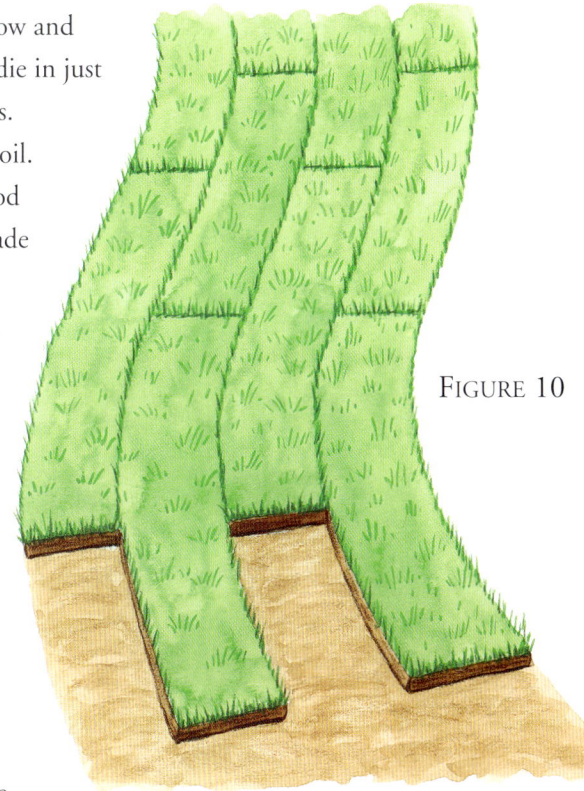

FIGURE 10

GARDEN PATHS & WALKWAYS

Sowing Grass Seed

If you're growing your path from seed, consider renting a drop-seeder to sow it; it will give you much more even and accurate results. The recommended distribution for grass seed varies according to species, but the instructions that accompany your seeds should tell you what setting to use on the drop-seeder.

After sowing the seeds, mix them into the top ¼ inch of soil by raking the entire path. Fill a lawn roller halfway with water and roll the seeded soil. Finish by mulching the path with straw or hay; this will help keep the soil moist while the seeds germinate.

Creating a Grass Path in an Existing Lawn

In addition to laying sod and sowing seeds, there's another way you can make a grass path: by transforming your existing lawn into a winding path, edged with flower and herb beds. Start by deciding where your path will be and where the beds will be. Then mark the path, as described on pages 20 and 21. Cut the turf all along the path's border with a shovel or an edger. Using a foot adz hoe, mattock, flat-nosed shovel, or a sod cutter, remove the sod from the areas that will be flower beds. Set edging along the path (see page 27), making sure the edging material protrudes no more than 1 inch above ground level; otherwise, you'll have to hand trim

your path! Till and fertilize the soil in the flower beds as needed; then add the flowers and herbs of your choice.

Maintenance

Your local agricultural extension office will be able to tell you how often you should mow and fertilize sod to keep it healthy in your type of soil. If you grow your path from seed, you may mow it when the seedlings are about 3 inches high; just make sure the soil isn't too wet and that the mower blades are very sharp; dull blades can cause the mower to pull the grass out by its fragile roots. Give a seed-grown path about five weeks before treading on it. After that, care for it exactly as you would care for your lawn.

CUT STONE

Additional Tools and Materials

- Graph paper, pencil, and copy machine
- Circular saw equipped with a masonry blade, scrap 2 x 4 to use as a cutting guide, safety glasses, and ear plugs (optional, you'll only need these items if you have to cut your stone, see pages 110 through 112)
- Garden hose with spray nozzle

FINISHING YOUR PATH   33

For mortaring cut stone, you'll also need:

- Trowel
- Mortar (a mix of one part Portland cement to three or four parts sand works well)
- Coloring agent for mortar (optional, available where you buy cement)
- Damp sponge or rag

Whether you're dry-laying your path or mortaring the stones in place, start by sketching your path layout to scale on a piece of standard graph paper. Use a copy machine to enlarge the sketch and to make several copies. Then familiarize yourself with the shapes and sizes in which stone is available in your area. Visualize the patterns you can create. Then try various patterns on the enlarged sketches. If this step sounds tedious to you, keep in mind that erasing a misplaced stone will be much quicker—and easier on your back—than moving a real one! Sketching your path and pattern to scale will also help you determine how much stone to order. Figure 11 on the following page shows a few possible patterns for cut stone paths.

As you work on your path's pattern, keep a few design tips in mind:

- In a random pattern with different sizes of stones, use smaller stones in the path's interior where they'll be less likely to dislodge; use larger stones on the edges and at the beginning and end to stabilize the path.

- Smaller stones require a more stable foundation, so if your stones are all particularly small or brittle, consider mortaring them in place (preferably on a concrete base), rather than dry-laying them.

- Even with cut stone, the edges will rarely fit together perfectly, so count on leaving spaces of between ¼ and ¾ inch between stones. Leave larger spaces if you'd like to incorporate herbs or other plants in your walkway.

- Consider mixing cut stone with other materials, such as gravel, brick, or tile.
- If your path leads from one structure to another, use your most attractive stones closest to the buildings.
- You can trim or cut stone to fit your pattern, if necessary. See page 110-111 for directions.

Dry-Laying Cut Stone

The top 1-inch layer of sand on a gravel base makes an excellent dry bed for laying stone. You can also add a 1-inch layer of sand to a concrete bed and dry-lay cut stone on it. Naturally, stones settle downhill, so if your path is on a slope, start laying your stones (according to your pattern) at the low end. Then work your way up. Set a few stones at a time, working them back and forth in the sand until you like the arrangement. Check the slope with your level. The best way to do this is to lay a board or a length of 2 x 4 across the stones, and place the level on top of that. This way, you can determine the slope of a portion of the path, not just an individual stone in it.

Continue laying the stones, a few at a time, until the path is complete. Sweep sand into the gaps between the stones; it should come to about ¼ inch below the path surface. Use a hose with a spray nozzle to thoroughly wet the entire path surface and the sand. Walk over the stones to help settle them. You may need to add more sand at this point so that it's still at the ¼-inch level.

Mortaring Cut Stone

If you're mortaring over a concrete base, let the cement set at least overnight before starting. When you're ready to start laying the stones, prepare some mortar. (If you'd like your mortar to match or accent your stone, use some coloring agent, available where cement is sold.) Use a trowel to spread a 1-inch layer of it over the base. Using your pattern as a guide, set the stones in place. Fill the gaps between the stones with additional mortar. Use a damp cloth or sponge to clean off any mortar that gets on the top surface of the stones. Allow the

FIGURE 11

Sample designs for paths made from cut stone

FINISHING YOUR PATH 35

mortar to set at least a day before walking on the path.

Maintenance

To maintain a dry-laid cut-stone path, check the sand level throughout the year, and add more as necessary. You may also need to rework the stone if it buckles or inches out of place. Keep an eye out for tree roots, and trim them back before they become a problem. If you don't want vegetation on your path, you'll probably need to weed occasionally. A mortared cut-stone path should be virtually maintenance free.

NATURAL STONE

Additional Tools and Materials

- Brick chisel and mason's hammer (for cutting and trimming stone, see pages 110 through 112)
- Hose with spray nozzle

For mortaring natural stone, you'll also need:

- Trowel
- Mortar (a mix of one part Portland cement to three or four parts sand works well)
- Coloring agent for mortar (optional, available where you buy cement)
- Damp sponge or rag

Before you purchase your stone, spend some time at your path site visualizing the kinds of patterns that would work well. You can set natural stone in gravel; fit it together tightly like a jigsaw puzzle; arrange it into stepping stones (see pages 29 and 30 for information about laying stepping-stone paths); plant between it with herbs, grass, or moss; or try any other kind of design that suits your site. Let your imagination—and your site—guide you. After you've decided on a basic pattern and design, you'll have a better idea of how much and what kind of stone to buy. Figure 12 on the following page shows a few possible patterns for natural-stone paths.

Dry-Laying Natural Stone

Lay your stones directly on the top, 1-inch sand layer of the path base. Start with the stones that will form the outer edges of the path; in general, these border stones should be relatively large. Work in from the edges, placing the smaller stones toward the path's center. You may need to cut or trim some of your stones to fit better;

GARDEN PATHS & WALKWAYS

Figure 12

Large natural stones, dry-laid on sand

Small natural stones, mortared

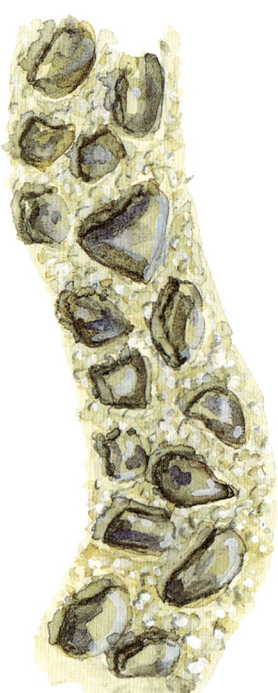
Large natural stones, dry-laid in gravel

Large natural stones along edges, and small stones in the interior

the techniques are described on pages 110 through 112. Try to leave at least ¾ inch between each stone to allow for better drainage. Don't settle the stones into the sand yet, though.

After you've paved a few feet of the path, check your design. You may want to adjust the stones. When you're happy with the arrangement, settle the stones by working them back and forth in the sand with your hands. Then give each one a few taps with a rubber mallet. For better drainage, the stones' top surfaces should be about ½ inch above the surrounding ground. Make sure the stones are as level as possible.

Continue laying the path, working on a few feet at a time. When all the stones are in place, pour sand into the gaps to about ½ inch below the path surface. Wet the path thoroughly; then walk back and forth on it to settle the stones. Check the sand in the gaps and add more, if necessary, to bring its level back to ½ inch.

Mortaring Natural Stone

Simply follow the same process described for mortaring a path of cut stone. (See page 34.)

Maintenance

To maintain a path of dry-laid natural stone, weed it when necessary and level stones that move or heave during the year. If you're growing plants in your path, be sure to keep them watered as needed. Other than the occasional sweeping, mortared natural stone should require almost no maintenance.

BRICK

Additional Tools and Materials

- Brick sett (see page 113), mason's hammer, and safety glasses; or, if you have a number of bricks to cut, a rented brick saw, gloves, safety glasses, and earphones
- Small piece of plywood to use as a kneeling board

For dry-laying brick, you'll also need:

- Garden hose and adjustable spray nozzle

FIGURE 13

Diagonal Running Board *Herringbone* *Basketweave* *Brick and Tile*

For mortaring brick, you'll also need:

- Trowel
- Mortar (a mix of one part Portland cement to three or four parts sand works well)
- Coloring agent for mortar (optional, available where you buy cement)
- Damp sponge or rag

Building a brick path requires a little more planning than building other types of paths. Take time to find a pattern you like and are comfortable laying, especially if you decide to mortar the bricks in place. With some effort, you can rework dry-laid bricks; reworking mortared brick, however, is more of a job than most people want. Figure 13 shows some common patterns for a brick path.

Dry-Laying Brick

If you're paving over a concrete base, add a 1-inch layer of sand first. Then install sturdy edging to keep the bricks in place. Pressure-treated 2 x 4 lumber or commercial-grade metal or plastic edging work well. Use a hose and an adjustable spray nozzle (set to fine) to gently and evenly wet the sand on top of the base. Level the sand by dragging a screed over it.

Place your kneeling board in the sand, just ahead of where you want to begin. Resting your knees on the board, start laying the brick according to your pattern. Set each brick by tapping it with a rubber mallet. Check the bricks periodically with a level to make sure the path is even and has the proper degree of slope. After you've laid a few feet of path, sweep sand into the gaps between the bricks. Water the sand, then repeat until it fills the gaps almost flush with the tops of the bricks. Continue until you've completed the entire path.

Mortaring Brick

Make sure you're 100-percent happy with your design before you even think about getting started—because if you want to change it later, you'll have to tear out your entire path.

If you're mortaring over a concrete base, allow cement to set overnight or longer. Then mix your mortar. You may want to add some coloring agent so it matches or complements your brick. Use a trowel to spread a ¾-inch layer of mortar over the base. Start laying the brick according to your pattern. Stop to check the pattern and the brick's grade every few feet. Correct any problems now before the mortar sets. When you're happy with a segment of path, fill the gaps between the bricks with mortar. Use the trowel to smooth the mortar in the gaps. Working quickly, use a damp sponge or rag to wipe off any mortar that gets on the top surfaces of the brick. Allow the path to set for at least 24 hours before walking on it.

Maintenance

Tree roots and hard freezes can buckle dry-laid brick, so you may need to rework portions of your path from time to time. Sweep more sand into the gaps between the bricks when the sand level gets low, and pull weeds that try to sprout before they become deeply rooted. A well-laid mortared brick path shouldn't require more than an occasional sweeping.

FINISHING YOUR PATH   39

CONCRETE

Additional Tools and Materials

- Scrap lumber, wooden stakes, hammer, and nails (for creating form boards)
- Expansion-joint strips (available where you buy cement)
- Bagged, premixed cement; or Portland cement, sand, and gravel (A mix of one part Portland cement, two and a half parts sand, and four parts gravel works well for a path.)
- Cement mixer, or wheelbarrow and hoe
- Garden hose and adjustable spray nozzle
- Plastic sheeting

Concrete can be dressed up in dozens of creative ways: You can make your own pavers by pouring cement into molds, or buy pre-made concrete pavers; create and a lay a design with either kind the same way you would if you were working with brick. Give poured concrete a funky new hue with a coloring agent; embed it with decorative pebbles; embellish it with ceramic tiles; or add your family's footprints to it. However you decide to personalize your concrete path, be sure you're satisfied with the design—before you pour the concrete! The only way to change it after the fact is to tear up the whole path. Just to be sure, try your design ideas in a test box first. Nail together four 1-foot-long pieces of 2 x 6 lumber in the shape of a box. Place the box on a sheet of plywood that's resting on level ground. Mix a small batch of concrete and pour it in. Then experiment with every wacky idea you can think up! Figure 14 on the following page shows just a few options for livening up a concrete path.

For a concrete path, the base doubles as the path itself. This means you won't have to dig the base as deep—only about 4 inches, compared to the standard 7 to 8 inches for a concrete base destined to be topped with another material.

Start by preparing the soil and placing form boards as described in the section on pouring a concrete base (pages 24 and 25). The top edges of the form boards should come up to the path's surface level. Strengthen them by attaching them at their joints with "splice boards"; these are just scrap pieces of lumber, nailed to the outside faces of the form boards.

40 GARDEN PATHS & WALKWAYS

FIGURE 14

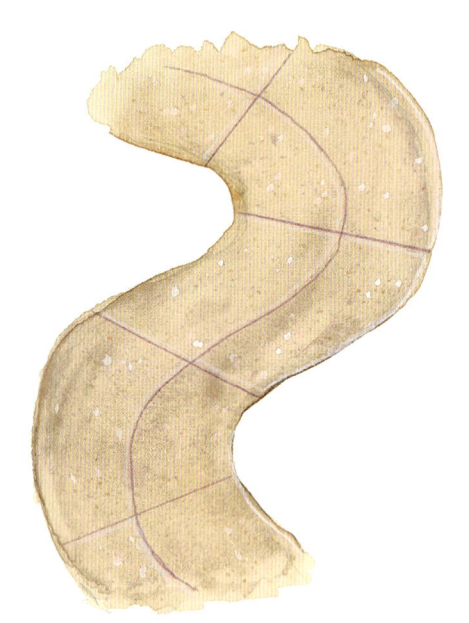

Curving path of concrete, tinted for added interest

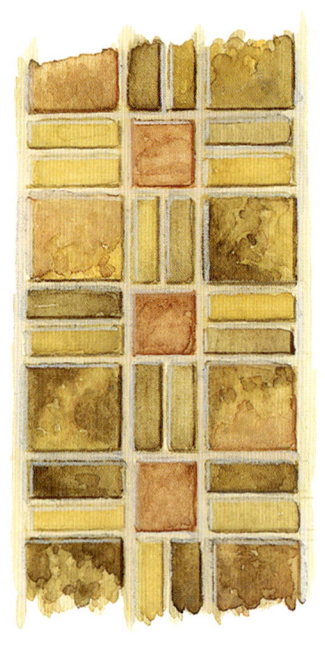

Concrete pavers laid in a formal pattern

Concrete embedded with colorful bits of tile

Concrete embedded with small gravel

Because concrete will expand and contract with temperature fluctuations, it's prone to cracking, buckling, and surface chipping. Fortunately, you can help prevent these problems with expansion-joint strips. These are strips of fiber board, impregnated with asphalt or another material that will expand and compress with temperature changes. Cut the strips to length and place them across your path bed at 12-foot intervals; they should fit snugly between the form boards. Also use them at any point where the path abuts a structure or curves sharply.

Prepare your concrete. You can mix small amounts right in your wheelbarrow. For larger amounts, consider renting a gas-powered cement mixer, or having ready-to-pour cement delivered right to your house. If you're mixing your own concrete, test its consistency by pouring a small amount into the path base and running your trowel across it; the surface should be smooth and glistening. If the surface is too runny or watery, add more dry cement. If it's rough, add more water, a little at a time.

Pour the concrete into the path base. Working quickly, use a shovel or a hard iron rake to push the concrete into place. Smooth the concrete to an even finish by pulling a screed back and forth across it. You may want to enlist a friend or a family member to help with the screed; that way, you can have one person at each end. Use a float to give the surface a final smoothing.

Even with expansion-joint strips, concrete still may crack in harsh weather. By adding control joints, you can encourage the path to break cleanly at planned intervals. To make control joints, use your edging tool and a scrap of lumber as a guide to score ½-inch-deep lines across the entire width of your path at intervals of no more than 5 feet. Add the control joints right after working the path with a float.

To give your path extra interest, you can embed it with seashells, gravel, ceramic tiles, marbles, beach glass, or just about anything else you can think of. If you decide to embed objects in the path, mix, pour, screed, and float only a small amount of concrete at a time. Using rubber gloves to protect your hands, press the desired objects into the wet concrete. Then place a thin sheet of plywood over them and use it to carefully press the objects even with the path's surface. Another way to add texture to concrete is to work the slightly-set surface with a stiff-bristled broom.

If you got any mud on the concrete, wash it off quickly; otherwise, it will stain your path. While you're at it, hose yourself off, too; concrete will harden on your hands and clothes just as easily as in your path base. If you expect rain, cover the setting concrete with plastic sheeting. Let the path set for two days; then pull out the form boards. After four days, you may start putting your path to use.

Maintenance

An occasional sweeping is all it should take to keep your path looking its best.

Concrete pavers

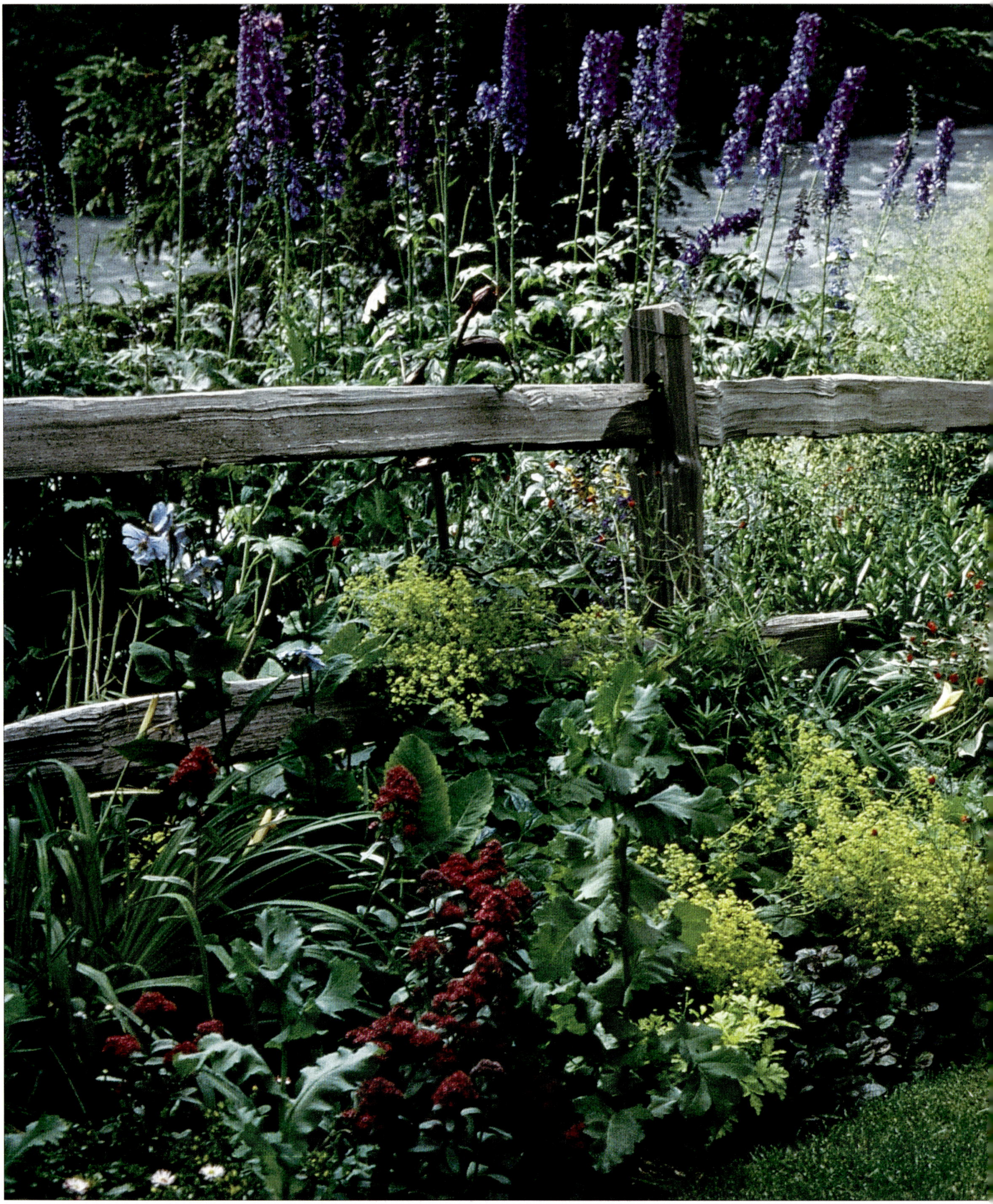

Garden Borders

Boundaries. We erect them to maintain our individuality in relationships; to mark the line between professional and private self; and, often, to define who we are as people. Garden borders—hedges, fences, and walls—serve many of the same functions, but in a much more direct and tangible way. A well-designed border declares that your home and family are part of a community; at the same time, it delineates your space from that of others.

Depending on the type of border you choose, it can also offer privacy, security, protection from the natural elements, and—of course—added charm and beauty.

Regardless of why you want a border, though, this chapter will help you decide what kind is best for your purposes. It will guide you through the process of planning where to place a border; then it will introduce you to the basic techniques required to grow a hedge, build a fence, and erect a wall. Then read about creating entries through your border. If you'd like to enhance the appearance of an existing hedge, fence, or wall, you'll find tips for doing that in the following pages, too.

You certainly can use a border as a simple demarcation of where your property begins and ends, but as you'll soon discover, it can be much more. So turn the page, open the gate, and come on in.

Choosing a Border

This stacked stone wall clearly establishes the boundary between lawn and patio.

Every border has a job to do, and probably more than just one. To select the right border for your outdoor space, start by identifying what you want it to accomplish. This section describes some common reasons for erecting borders, and includes some tips on what features make a border effective for a particular job.

TO ESTABLISH BOUNDARIES

A border's most basic function is simply to demarcate one space as separate from another, and almost any hedge, fence, or wall will serve in this capacity. For instance, a neat picket fence is a pretty reminder to passers-by that community property ends on their side of the slats.

TO CREATE PRIVACY

A border doesn't need to resemble a fortress to offer a measure of seclusion. As long as it reaches eye-level or higher, even an openwork fence will offer some privacy; the mere presence of a tall enclosure tends to discourage eyes from looking farther. For maximum privacy, however, choose a high, thick hedge, a solid wall of brick, or a fence with tightly spaced infill (see page 53).

Be warned, though: Solid borders will halt prying eyes, but they may also block wind a little too effectively, resulting in strong down drafts and miniature wind tunnels at entryways.

TO MITIGATE THE ELEMENTS

The best borders for mitigating natural elements have small openings: fences with closely spaced infill (see page 53), openwork brick walls, lush hedges. These borders diffuse, rather than block, the sun and wind. The result? Cool, partial shade without unwanted down drafts or turbulence.

Although the average backyard fence or hedge won't significantly dull the din of traffic, it will block your view of cars and other noise-makers—thereby dulling your perception of the racket. On the other hand, a thick, well-built wall can actually stop some sound waves; however, the design and construction of walls that are thick enough and tall enough to be truly soundproof is best left to landscape architects and engineers.

TO SECURE AND CONTAIN

Throughout history, borders have prevented unwanted guests from getting in, and kept selected inhabitants from getting out. Fortunately your garden border doesn't need to reach the proportions of the Great Wall of China to perform the same functions. A border's deterring effect is often more psychological than physical: The mere presence of one tells people that entrance is by invitation only. And while keeping very young children in may require actual physical obstacles, older children usually understand, when told, that the border marks the outer limit of where they can explore without your permission or company.

For more serious security, a very basic principle applies: The higher and stronger the border, the more effective a barrier it will be. As long as its style and finish harmonize with your home, even a very secure border can appear gracious. Although they're not discussed in this book, professionally installed security systems are also an option.

TO ENHANCE YOUR HOME

Some borders have the sole purpose of looking good. And by looking good, a fence, hedge, or wall can make your home and property look better, too. The best-looking borders both contrast with and complement the structures they surround. The key is to find one element in your home's design and incorporate that element in your border. Maybe your shutters are painted a particular shade of off-white; painting your fence that color, too, would tie your property together in a pleasing way.

Border Heights

Note: Many communities have restrictions on border heights and styles. Be sure to check with your local building department before installing any kind of border.

PURPOSE	MINIMUM HEIGHT	COMMENTS AND SUGGESTIONS
To contain or deter dogs	60 inches	A chain-link fence may not be the most attractive border, but it can withstand chewing and scratching. It will also allow you to keep an eye on your pet.
To contain or deter cats	60 inches	Choose a border that discourages climbing, such as a solid wall or a vertically planned, wooden board fence.
To deter deer and other wildlife*	72 inches and up	Make your border highly visible by using brightly colored material or by painting it. See page 77 for more information about deer.
To contain children up to 3 years old	48 inches	A childproof border should be free from hand holds, splinters, thorns, and sharp points. Brick walls are a good option.
To contain children up to 10 years old	60 to 72 inches	Vertically planned wooden board, metal chain-link, and wooden basket-weave fences are all good choices for containing older children.
To provide privacy	72 inches and up	Tall lattice-work fences overgrown with vines offer privacy without making you feel closed in. Hedges are another good option, because community restrictions on fence and wall heights often don't apply to trees and shrubs.
To buffer noise	72 inches and up	Masonry walls are the best choice. Tall, thick hedges and solid wooden fences will also provide some buffering.
To provide security	72 inches and up	Any tall, heavy fence or wall that doesn't provide hand holds will discourage most would-be trespassers. Thick hedges with thorns are a good choice, too. Secure the gates or entries with padlocks or dead-bolt locks.

*High borders obviously won't deter burrowing wildlife, such as moles and groundhogs. You'll have to stop these pests below the ground. The concrete footing of a masonry wall will discourage most burrowers; however, if you're building a fence, attach kickboards made from 2 x 10 lumber between the fence posts, several inches below ground. See pages 76 and 77 for more information on deterring wildlife.

Where to Put Your Border

Whether you're installing a hedge, fence, or a wall, to do the job you want it to do, a border must be sited in the right location. You probably already have a general idea of where you'd like your border to be, but when you build a more or less permanent structure, you need to be as exact as possible about its location—before you begin building it!

LEGAL CONSIDERATIONS

Start with the legalities: building codes and property lines. Your community may have restrictions on the type and style of structure you can build. Check with the local building inspector to learn about your community's regulations.

Then find the exact location of your property lines. The bank or other institution that holds your mortgage may have a boundary map of your property in their files. Check with the local building department, too. Ideally, you should have legal documentation of where your property begins and ends before erecting a border anywhere near its boundaries. For whatever reason, though, you may not be able to obtain that documentation. Although you should always discuss building plans with your immediate neighbors, this step becomes imperative if you don't have legal proof of your property lines. Whether you have documentation or not, consider formalizing your plans—and your neighbors' assent to them—in a written agreement. If this isn't possible, plan to set your border at least 6 inches back from the property line.

This well-placed fence offers privacy to neighbors on both sides.

MAPPING IT OUT

After you've determined where you can legally build your border, experiment with different placements and configurations. Will your planned fence, indeed, hide the shopping center in the distance? Or will it do more to block your view of the evening sunset? The easiest way to find out is to try your ideas on a site plan of your home and property.

If your house is fairly new, the local building department may have a site plan for it on file; or, if you've had your property professionally landscaped recently, your landscape architect will probably have one. Otherwise, you can easily draw a site plan yourself, as described below. Then work with your site plan manually, or use one of the many landscaping software programs available for homeowners.

CREATING AND USING A SITE PLAN

Start by making a sketch of your lot, including all your property's important features: property lines; the house and other structures, such as sheds and existing borders; entrances to and from your home; gardens and flower beds; paths and walkways; patios; recreation areas; and anything else that might be relevant to the new border. Then enlist the help of a friend or family member and a 100-foot measuring tape; take measurements of all the features you sketched, including distances between features. Be sure to measure the perimeter around your property, too. Record the measurements right on your sketch.

Next, turn your sketch into a to-scale drawing. To do this manually, transfer your measurements and the property lines to a piece of ¼-inch graph paper, designating one square on the paper as equal to 2 feet, or another distance that suits your site. Figure 1 shows a typical hand-drawn site plan. If you're working with landscaping software, input the information as required by the particular program.

LAYING OUT THE BORDER

At this point, you should have a good representation of your property and a clear idea of the functions you want your border to perform. Use both to create the layout for your border. Start by "mapping" your priorities on the site plan. Indicate where the border will need to be to perform each function. For instance, if you hope to block a certain view, indicate the source of that view on your rendering. Other considerations you should mark include the path the sun travels over your property; the prevalent wind direction; traffic routes, both foot and vehicular; the source(s) of unwanted noise; and activity areas—where the kids normally play, the dog's territory, the stretch of lawn that hosts the croquet set, etc. By mapping all of these factors, you'll be able to see how a border will affect each one.

Next, experiment with different layouts for your border. Make several copies of your site plan so you can try more than one idea. Keep revising and experimenting until you've found a layout that satisfies your needs. Be sure to plan for gates and entries, too. (For more information about entryways, see pages 66 through 67.) As you work, keep track of dimensions; a good layout sketch with dimensions may help you estimate the amount material you'll need.

Once you've finalized where you want your border(s), you're ready to head outside and get to work.

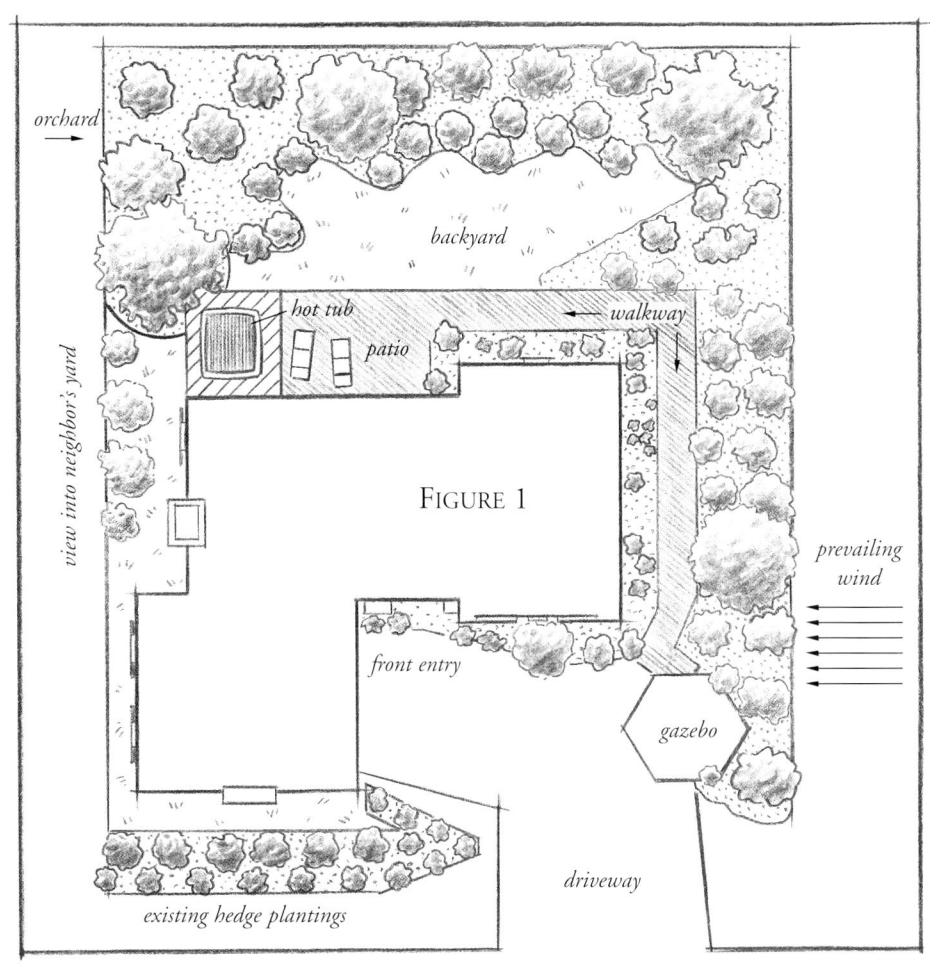

FIGURE 1

A site plan should show all of your property's important features.

Hedges

Hedges make excellent garden borders. Grown to heights of 6 feet and taller, they provide almost complete privacy; grown from dense, thorny shrubs, they'll provide a good deal of security, too. They're perfect windbreaks, filtering gusts rather than totally blocking or diverting them. Even a low hedge will clearly mark the boundaries of your property, direct traffic where you want it to go, and define and shape your outdoor space.

Hedges can be designed and grown to complement any style of home. They can be lightly pruned for a natural, informal look, or heavily pruned into geometric shapes for a more formal appearance. Trees and shrubs appropriate for hedges come in a huge variety of colors and textures, so you can choose plants with hues that match or complement your house and property.

Compared to fences and stone or brick walls, hedges are relatively easy and inexpensive to "install"—even on hilly or rolling sites. Laying out a hedge is also much less demanding than laying out a fence or wall. The project on pages 50 through 51 will walk you through the process of planting a hedge. However, if you'd like your living wall to follow perfectly straight lines and turn exact right angles, just follow the directions for laying out a fence line on pages 54 through 55.

Hedges aren't right for everyone, though. They take several years to reach the desired height, and they require more maintenance than other garden borders. All hedges, whether formal or informal, require regular pruning. Additionally, most need to be watered during dry spells. And unlike other garden borders, hedges can grow beyond their original boundaries, onto your neighbor's property. If your neighbor agrees to share ownership and maintenance of the hedge, this shouldn't be a problem. However, neighbors move, and your new ones may not be as willing to water and prune their side as your former neighbors were. To be safe, leave enough room between your hedge and your neighbors' property lines to accommodate the mature height and width of the plants you select with a set back of 6 inches.

CHOOSING PLANTS FOR YOUR HEDGE

To select the best plant(s) for your hedge, ask yourself a few questions:

- Do you want a hedge that's formal or informal? For a formal hedge, choose a slower-growing evergreen plant with dense, twiggy growth and small leaves or short needles. For a more informal border, you may want to select a variety of plants, including deciduous trees and shrubs with showy flowers or attractive fall foliage. The chart on page 51 offers suggestions for common plants for formal and informal hedges.

- Will children play near your hedge? If so, avoid thorny or toxic plants.

- How tall and how wide do you want your fully grown hedge to be, and how fast do you want it to reach those dimensions? Check the mature size of the plants you select and their rate of growth. Keep in mind that although fast-growing plants will yield a full-grown hedge sooner than a slower growing variety, they'll also require much more frequent pruning.

- Finally, consider the growing conditions at your site. What kind of soil does it have? How much sun and rain does it receive? Is it exposed to a lot of car traffic and pollution? Consult the staff at your local nursery to find plants that will grow well in the conditions at your site.

When you purchase your plants, choose small, young trees and shrubs rather than large, container-grown plants. In addition to being less expensive, younger plants generally experience less transplant shock, so they'll grow more quickly.

Planting a Hedge

FIGURE 2

Although you can choose from a wide variety of hedge plants and styles, the technique for planting a hedge of any kind is essentially the same. Most hedge plants will need to be watered on a weekly basis for the first two growing seasons. Check with your local nursery or plant supplier for recommendations about your specific plant(s) and site.

MATERIALS AND TOOLS

- Hedge plants (see chart on the facing page for suggestions)
- Tape Measure
- Stakes
- Mason's twine
- Shovel
- Pruning shears
- Drip hose (optional)
- Organic mulch

1 Start by laying out where you want your hedge. Mark each end of the site with a stake. Then, for a straight hedge, tie a string taut between the stakes. For a curving hedge, use a garden hose, twine, or inverted marking paint to indicate the hedge's path between the stakes.

2 Find the length of the hedge. For a straight hedge, measure the distance between the stakes. For a curving hedge, measure the length of the hose, twine, or line of inverted marking paint. Calculate the number of plants you'll need by dividing the length of the hedge by the recommended plant spacing. For instance, a 30-foot-long hedge grown from English yew—which should be planted about 2 feet apart—would require 15 plants.

3 Inspect the roots of each plant, pruning any that are damaged or broken. If you bought container-grown plants or balled-and-burlapped plants, remove and discard the container or burlap first; then loosen the roots if they're tight. Be sure to keep them moist.

4 Measure the spread and length of the plants' roots. Then dig a trench along the entire hedge line, as deep as the length of the roots and twice as wide as their spread.

5 Place the plants along the centerline of the trench according to the recommended spacing. The upper roots should be 1 inch below ground level. Measure the space between each plant as you go, adjusting as necessary; correcting the spacing at this point will be much easier than adjusting the plants after they're all in place.

6 Fill the trench halfway with soil, lightly packing the dirt around the roots. Water the soil thoroughly, and allow it to drain. Finish filling the trench; then water it again, using low water pressure or a drip hose to allow the moisture to soak in.

7 Add a 2- to 4-inch layer of organic mulch around the plants, but don't let any touch the plants' trunks or branches (this will help discourage pests and disease).

Plants for Hedges

The following plants work well in a formal hedge:

PLANT	FOLIAGE	HARDINESS ZONE	SUN REQUIREMENTS	PLANTING DISTANCE	PRUNING
English holly	Evergreen	7–9	FULL SUN TO PARTIAL SHADE	18 inches	Once a year, in late summer
Boxwood	Evergreen	5–9, depending on species	PARTIAL SHADE	12 inches	Twice a year, during summer
Hornbeam	Deciduous	4–8	FULL SUN TO PARTIAL SHADE	18 inches	Once a year, in late summer
European beech	Deciduous	5–7	PARTIAL SHADE	18 inches	Once a year, in late summer
English yew	Evergreen	7–8	FULL SUN TO FULL SHADE	24 inches	Twice a year, in summer and in autumn

The following plants work well in an informal hedge:

PLANT	FOLIAGE	HARDINESS ZONE	SUN REQUIREMENTS	PLANTING DISTANCE	PRUNING
Doublefile viburnum	Deciduous	4–8	FULL SUN TO PARTIAL SHADE	36 to 60 inches	Lightly, once a year in midspring
Glossy abelia	Evergreen or semi-evergreen	6–9	FULL SUN TO PARTIAL SHADE	24 to 48 inches	Lightly, once a year in midspring
Cherry laurel	Evergreen	6–9	FULL SUN TO PARTIAL SHADE	24 to 48 inches	Lightly, once a year in late spring

Note: For a formal hedge, buy all your plants from one supplier. Ask for matched plants from the same stock and of approximately the same size and age. Buy a few extras, too. Plant them nearby so you'll have replacements in case something happens to one of the plants in the hedge. Informal hedges don't need to look as if they're grown from a single plant, so you can purchase trees and shrubs for them from a variety of suppliers.

Fences

By strict definition, the word "fence" refers to any boundary or barrier. When we think of fences, however, we usually imagine rustic post-and-rails, utilitarian barbed wire, or homey pickets: boundaries created from wood, metal, or—in recent years—vinyl. They're more permanent-seeming than hedges, but less imposing than walls; easier and less expensive to install than brick, stone, or block, but more difficult and costly than neat rows of shrubbery.

Fences run the gamut of styles, construction techniques, and functions, but most follow a few general principles: Almost all fences share a basic anatomy, they can all be laid out the same way, and they all require postholes. So although this section focuses on traditional wooden fences, the information presented here can be used to build or install most other styles, too.

FENCE ANATOMY

All fences are constructed from a series of sections called "bays." A bay is made up of three parts: the footings, the framework, and the infill. Figure 3 on the following page shows a typical bay.

Footings

Footings anchor fence posts in the ground. And like anything that's anchored in the ground, fence posts are subject to some degree of frost-heave. Two common types of footings—gravel-and-earth and concrete—can help combat frost-heave and keep your fence posts upright and in alignment. Both are shown in figure 4.

Gravel-and-earth footings will hold fence posts steady in normal, stable soil. If your fence is less than 6 feet tall or not under a lot of stress, gravel-and-earth footings can still be appropriate, even in slippery clay or shifting sand. Postholes for this kind of footing should be twice the diameter of the posts. To calculate the depth, divide the aboveground height of the post by three; then add 4 to 6 inches for the gravel bed at the bottom.

More stable than gravel-and-earth footings, concrete footings are recommended for sites with strong winds and/or unstable soil, and for tall, solid, panel fences. They're also recommended for all gate and end posts, which are usually one dimension larger than the line posts. Concrete footings can keep your posts from rotting; just be sure to bury the last 2 inches of each post in a 4- to 6-inch gravel bed. The posthole for a concrete footing should be three times the width of the post. The depth for line posts is calculated the same way as for gravel-and-earth footings; for gate and end posts, add 12 inches to the line-post depth.

Consult a building inspector or fence builder in your area to determine which type of footing will work best at your site. If (s)he suggests concrete footings, ask for the recommended cement-sand-gravel ratio for your area.

Framework

The framework acts as the bay's skeleton, and is the structure to which the infill is fastened. It consists of posts—the vertical poles that link the fence to the ground and hold the bays upright; and rails—the horizontal crosspieces that join the posts.

In general, the posts should be set first before adding the rails. The rails can attach to the posts in a number of ways: They can fit into notches (*dadoes*) cut in the post faces, or in slots (*through mortises*) cut through the posts. They can be nailed directly to the posts, or fit snugly between them (as shown by the lower rails in figure 3). The upper rails

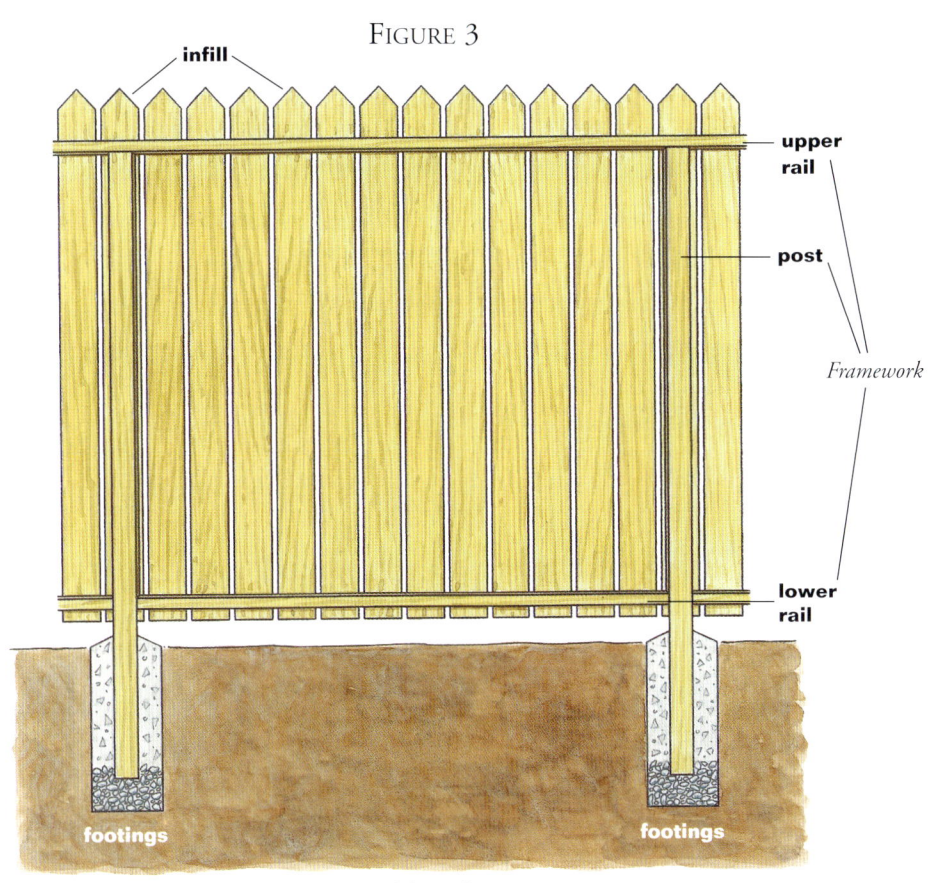

FIGURE 3

Typical fence bay

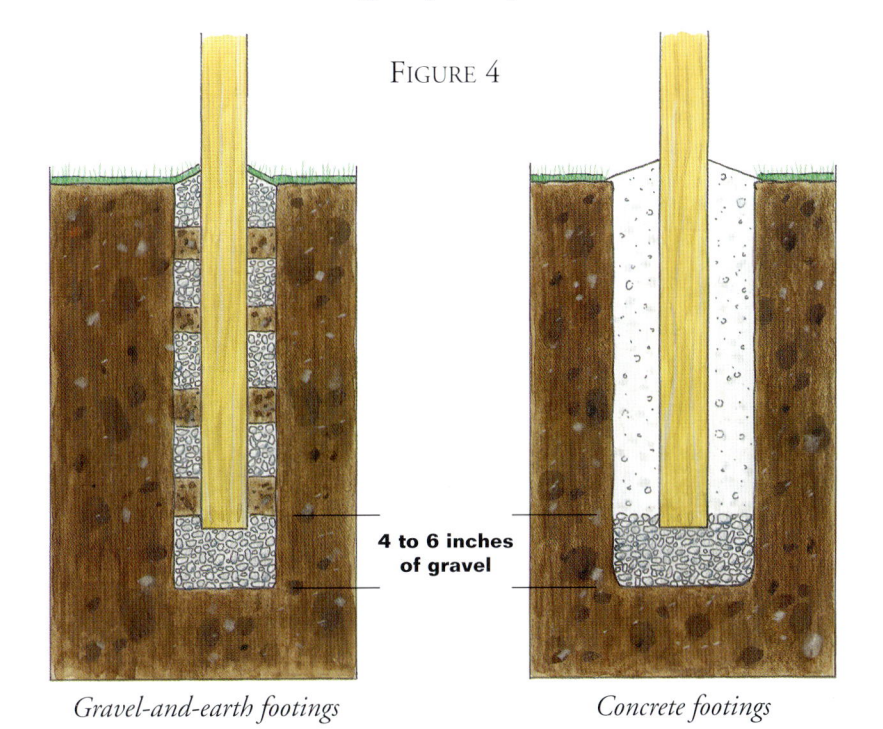

FIGURE 4

Gravel-and-earth footings

Concrete footings

can be attached in any of these ways, or they can run on top of the posts, as shown in figure 3. The length of the rails and the way you attach them will determine the on-center length of each bay, and thus the spacing of the postholes (see page 57).

If you're constructing fence bays yourself (rather than buying prefabricated fencing panels), design them to take advantage of standard lumber lengths such as 6, 10, or 12 feet; doing so will save you time, money, and wood. Consider the bay's proportions from an aesthetic perspective, too. In general, a perimeter fence will look best if its bays are twice as long as they are high. A formal fence enclosing a garden or a patio will look better if the bays are square.

Infill

The infill forms the fence's surface. Choices for infill range from the ubiquitous picket to the more exotic bamboo, and everything in between: plywood, glass, thermoplastic, vinyl, chain link, lattice panels, and anything else that can be fitted between or on the framework. Options for attaching infill to framework are just as varied, and will have as much impact on the fence's appearance and function as the material itself.

The project on pages 58 through 59 will show you how to build a classic picket fence from 96-inch-long bays with 4 x 4 line posts. Check the Internet and your local library for other fence designs, paying attention to the bay dimensions. If you're designing your own fence, sketch a sample bay on graph paper. You'll need to know how long each bay will be and the dimension of the fence posts in order to lay out the fence line, estimate materials, and dig the postholes.

LAYING OUT FENCE LINES

After you've established a design and layout on paper, transfer your plan to actual points on the ground. Although fences are the focus here, this plotting technique will work for laying out walls and hedges, too. Before you get started, take a good look at figure 5; it will give you a much better understanding of the procedure.

Start by cutting a supply of 24-inch lengths from 1 x 4 or 2 x 4 lumber. Sharpen one end of each length to a point to create stakes. For every two stakes you make, cut another 20-inch length of lumber to make crosspieces, leaving the ends square. (If you're building a wall, these crosspieces will need to be longer—see page 62.)

Use figure 5 as a guide to erect a batter board 3 feet beyond the terminal point of each section of fence line. (You can make construction easier by adjusting the distance between terminal points such that it's a multiple of the on-center length of your bays.) Drive the batter-board stakes into the ground first; then nail the crosspiece—one of the 20-inch lumber lengths—between. Tie a length of mason's twine taut between each set of crosspieces.

Check that the twine lines represent the layout you want. Make sure they're parallel to walls and other structures. To make adjustments, enlist a helper to move the twine laterally on the batter-board crosspieces while you check its position.

Borders that enclose rectangular or square areas should have 90-degree corners. To check for perpendicular, use the 3-4-5 triangle method shown in figure 5. At each corner, mark a point 3 feet out along one length of twine, and 4 feet out on the other piece. Measure the diagonal distance between the marks. The corner is 90 degrees when the distance is 5 feet. Mark or notch the crosspieces to mark the correct position of the lines.

DIGGING THE POSTHOLES

On flat sites, measure the distance between the location of each set of end posts, and divide that distance by the on-center length of your bays. If the distance isn't an exact multiple of your bay length, you can adjust the fence line, make two "half bays" at each end of the fence, or adjust the length of the bays; choose the method that works best for you.

Measure off your posthole locations and mark them on the twine line with bits of tape. Transfer the points to the ground with a plumb bob. Mark each point by driving a nail through a scrap of cloth at the exact point where the plumb bob landed. Loosen the lines to make space for digging the postholes.

If you marked postholes by measuring along the actual terrain on a sloped site, they would be too closely spaced. Use the following technique instead: Cut a 1 x 4 to the length of

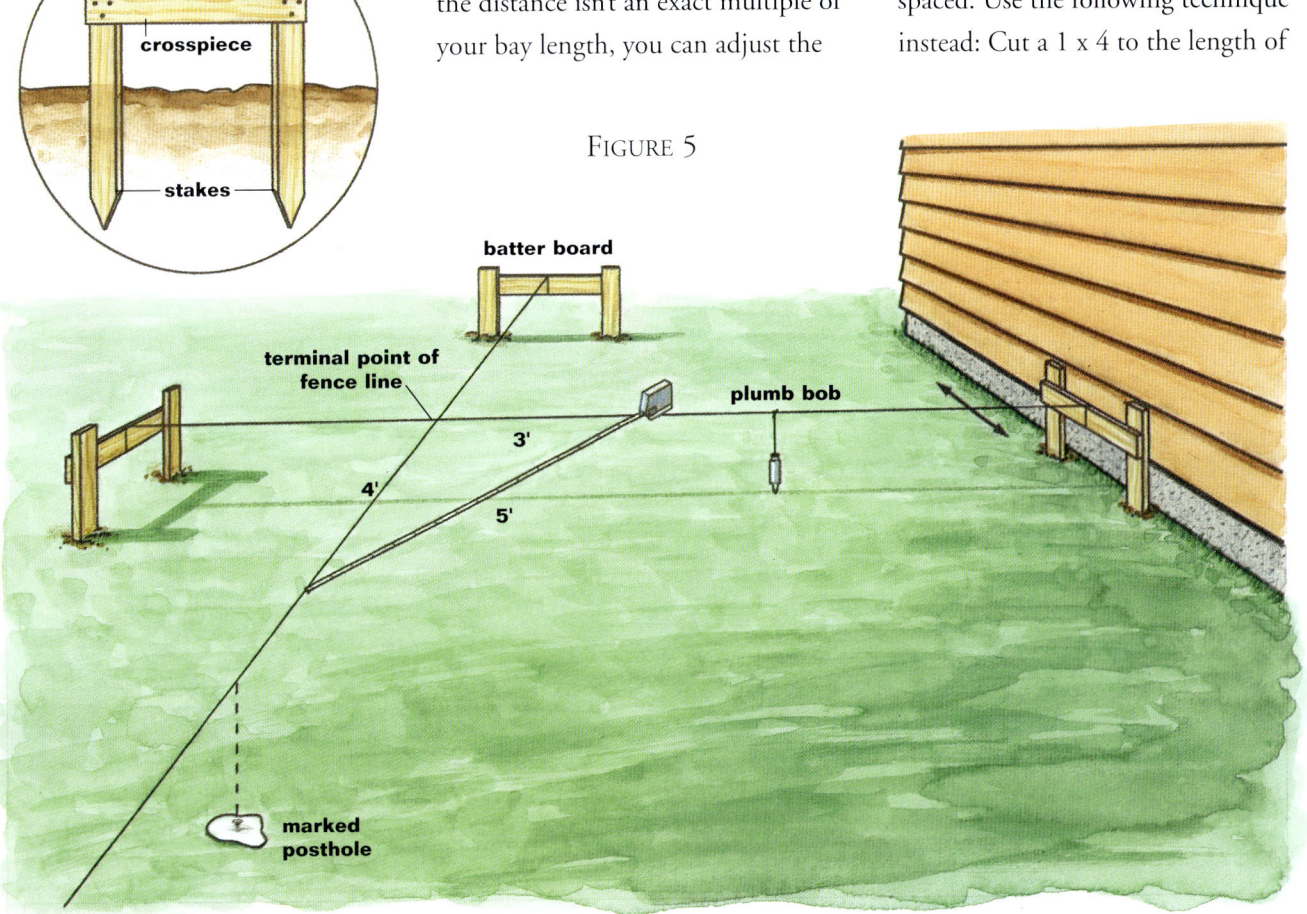

FIGURE 5

FIGURE 6

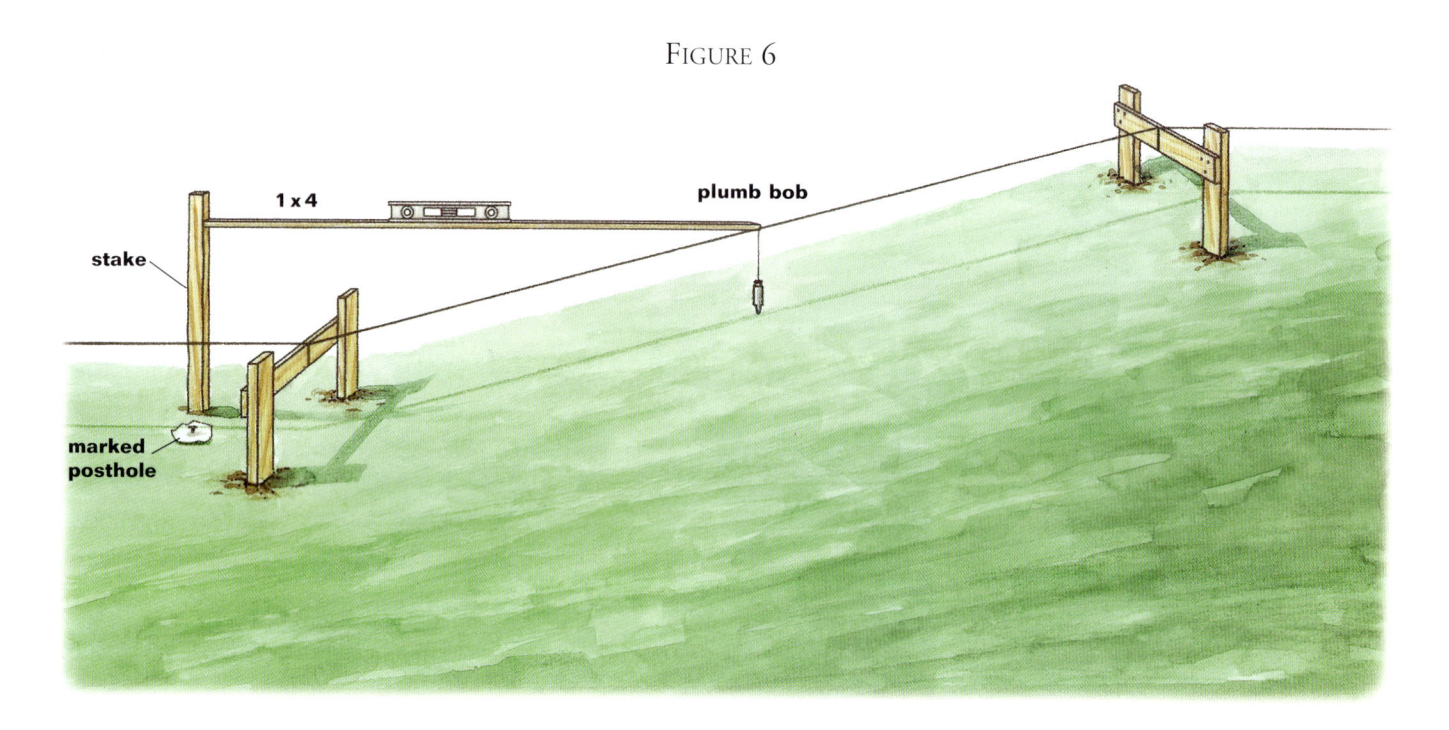

the necessary distance between postholes. Drive a stake into the earth, flush with the last posthole marker on flat ground. Grab a friend to help; then, using figure 6 as a guide, hold the 1 x 4 so one end butts up against the stake and the other end touches the twine line. Adjust the position of the 1 x 4 until it's level. Mark the spot with a plumb bob, cloth scrap, and a nail, just as you would on a level site.

Most professional fence builders suggest digging all your postholes at once. Most homeowners who have built fences suggest digging postholes as you go. The difference in opinion reflects a difference in experience. Professionals lay out fence lines on a daily basis; the average homeowner doesn't, and is therefore more likely to make miscalculations. If you're confident about your layout, dig the holes all at once; as long as your calculation are correct, you'll save time, and—if you've rented a posthole digger—money. If you don't feel confident, swallow the extra rental expense, and dig the holes as you build the fence.

Digging postholes isn't an easy job. Consider renting a power auger if you're digging more than a dozen; just make sure it will create the proper diameter hole (see pages 52 and 53). For smaller jobs, try a clamshell digger. Don't dig postholes with a shovel, though; it won't create the straight, clean sides necessary for setting fence posts. For loosening rocks, consider renting or buying a steel digging bar, too.

There's no one right way to dig a posthole, but there is a correct end result. A posthole should be dug exactly at the center of the point you flagged. It should be plumb, cut to the correct depth, and—ideally—wider at the base than at the top (this is where a clamshell digger comes in handy). Remove any loose earth from the bottoms of the holes. Then fill each hole with 4 to 6 inches of gravel.

Enlist someone to help you set the fence posts. Then adjust the fence line so the posts will fit inside: Measure the width of the posts, divide by two, and move the twine over that amount on the crosspiece of each batter board; the posts should fit just inside the line. (See figure 7.)

Install the end posts first. Place one in its hole and twist it to bury the end 2 inches in the gravel bed. Using figure 7 as a guide, nail 1 x 2 braces to opposite faces of the post. Check for plumb with a level. When the post is perfectly straight, drive a stake adjacent to each brace; then nail the brace to the stake to anchor the post in its plumb position. If you need to hold the post at a particular height, add cleats, too. (See figure 7.) Repeat to set the opposite end post.

String a second length of twine taut between the end posts, tying the ends to nails driven in the same face of the posts as the first length, about 12 inches from the top ends. This piece of twine will help you set the line posts in proper alignment. Place, align, and brace the line posts (exactly as you did the end posts) just inside—but not touching—the upper and lower twine lines.

Check the posts for plumb again, and make any necessary adjustments. Then add the footing material. For gravel-and-earth footings, add the layers in 6-inch increments, tamping each with a sturdy length of lumber before adding the next. Finish by forming a sloped collar around the post to help shed rain. (See figure 4 on page 53.) For concrete fill, work on one hole at a time. Shovel the cement in; then work a steel bar up and down to remove any air bubbles. Form a sloped cap at the top with a trowel. If you used gravel-and-earth footings, you may remove the braces now; if you used concrete footings, leave them in place for at least two days to allow the cement set.

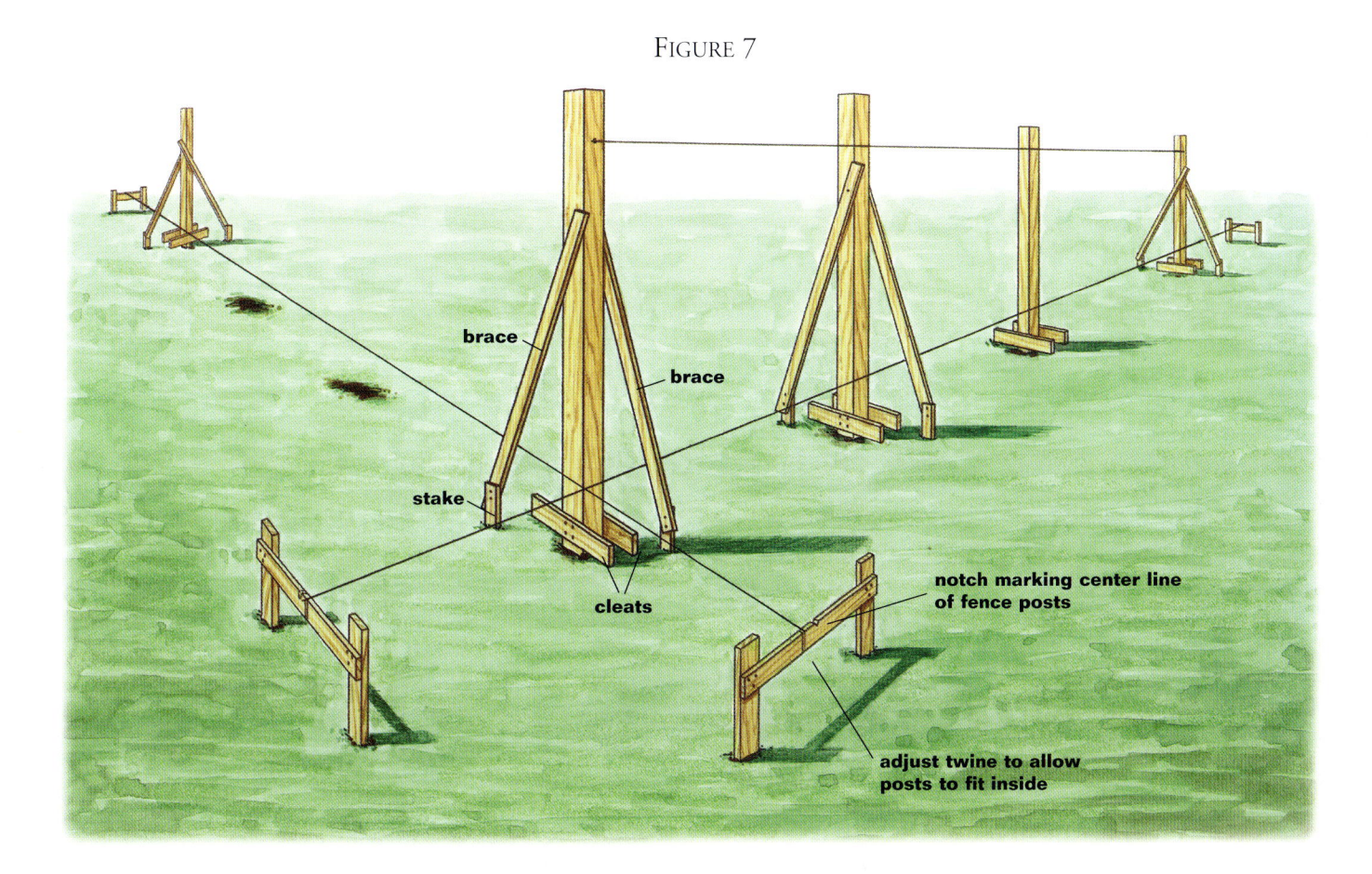

FIGURE 7

Building a Picket Fence

FIGURE 8

The classic picket is probably the most popular fence style of all, and with good reason; its simple good looks can be varied endlessly to suit any home. Use the general instructions here and the information on the previous pages to create a fence that's right for your site.

CUTTING LIST (for one 8'-long, 4'-high bay)

CODE	DESCRIPTION	QTY.	MATERIAL	DIMENSIONS
A	Line posts	2	4 x 4	66" long*
B	Lower rail	1	2 x 4	92½" long
C	Upper rail	1	2 x 4	192" long**
D	Pickets	16	1 x 4	46" long
E	Spacer	1	1 x 4	40" to 46" long, ripped to width (see step 4)

*This dimension assumes a 24"-deep posthole; your site may require deeper postholes and, therefore, longer posts.

**Each upper rail (C) spans three posts and meets the adjacent rail in the center of a post, so you'll only need one upper rail for every two bays.

MATERIALS AND TOOLS
(for one 8'-long, 4'-high bay)

- 11 linear feet 4 x 4 pressure-treated pine
- 25 linear feet 2 x 4 pressure-treated pine
- 70 linear feet 1 x 4 pressure-treated pine
- 4 #8 x 3" exterior deck screws
- 4 8d (2½") galvanized common nails
- 66 6d (2") galvanized common nails
- Tape measure and pencil
- Circular saw
- Power drill with #8 countersink and #8 pilot bit
- Phillips driver bit or Phillips-head screw driver
- Line level
- C-clamps
- 2' or 4' level

BUILDING A PICKET FENCE   59

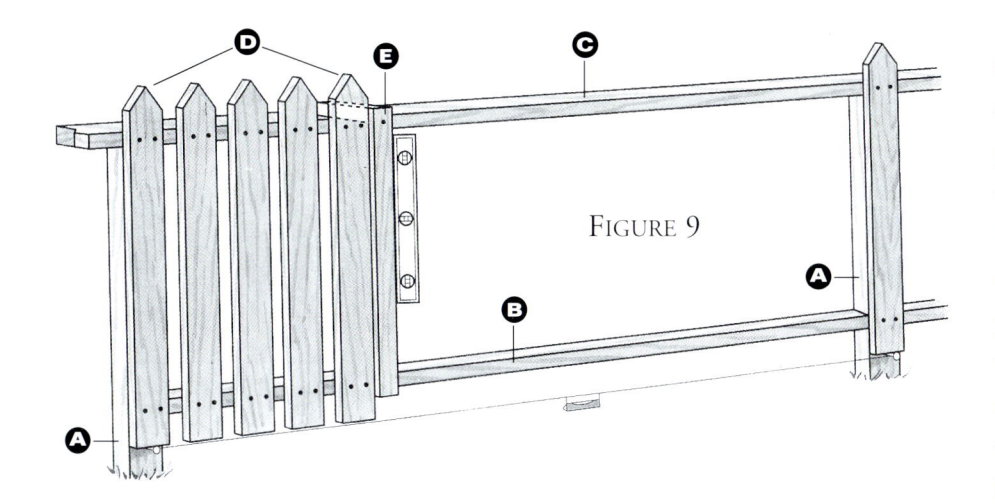

FIGURE 9

TIPS

- You'll also need a 78"-long piece of 6 x 6 pressure-treated pine for each end post. (This length assumes a posthole depth of 36 inches.)
- You can make the pickets yourself by sawing one end of each 46"-long 1 x 4 to a point, or you can buy precut pickets from a home improvement center.
- Simplify assembly by pre-boring all the joints for screws. (See page 97.)

Instructions

1 Set the posts as described on page 57. Then add the rails. To calculate the length of the bottom rail, hold a 2 x 4 in position against the posts and mark the cuts. Trim the 2 x 4 to size; then use C-clamps to hold it about 4 inches above the ground. Check the rail for plumb; then fasten it with two #8 x 3" screws at each joint—one angled through each narrow face. Attach the upper rail with two 8d nails through its top face at each joint.

2 Stretch a length of mason's twine taut and level between the posts at least 2 inches above ground level (see figure 9); this line will help you place the pickets at the proper height.

3 Clamp a picket against a post, edges flush. The picket's top should extend 6 inches beyond the top of the post, and its bottom should be even with the twine line. Attach the picket to the post with two 6d nails at each upper and lower rail location. Repeat to attach a picket to the opposite post.

4 The actual spacing of the pickets will vary slightly from bay to bay, but as long as they're spaced more or less equally within each bay, your fence will look fine. To determine the spacing within each bay, start by multiplying the number of pickets between the posts by the width of the pickets: 14 pickets times 3½ inches equals 49 inches—this is the total space occupied by the pickets. (Remember that the 1 x 4 pickets are actually 3½ inches wide—see page 118.) Subtract that number from the distance between the posts to calculate the total open space: 92½ inches minus 49 inches equals 43½ inches. Divide the open space by the number of spaces between pickets: 43½ inches divided by 15 spaces is equal to just under 3 inches per space. Make a spacer by ripping a board to that width. Nail a cleat to one end of the spacer so you can hang it from the top rail as you add the pickets. (See figure 9.)

5 Hang the spacer against one of the post pickets. Butt the next picket against the spacer, bottom end even with the twine line. Check it for plumb; then clamp the picket in place and attach it to the rails with two 6d nails through each joint. Repeat to attach the remaining pickets. Before adding the last few pickets, check the spacing to make sure it will come out evenly; if it doesn't, spread the discrepancy evenly over the remaining pickets in the bay.

Walls

Whether constructed from stone, brick, or any of the dozens of styles of commercially available block, walls are the most substantial and permanent type of garden border. Built high enough, a wall can provide almost complete privacy. Built thick enough, it can provide a great deal of peace and quiet, too.

Building a wall, however, is not a project to be undertaken casually. In general, walls are much more costly and time-consuming to erect than hedges or fences. Although dry-stacked stone walls require little more than well-tamped soil as a base, mortared walls must be built on proper footings. This section includes general instructions for constructing footings on level ground, but you'll need to consult your local building department to learn about codes specific to your area, and to obtain any permits that may be necessary. Finally, walls that exceed 3 feet in height require special design and building techniques, so if you'd like something taller, enlist professional help.

WALL MATERIALS

Stone, brick, and block are the most common choices for creating garden walls. The project on pages 64 through 65 will walk you through every step of building a mortared stone wall. However, if you'd like to build a dry-stacked stone wall or a wall from brick or block, visit your local library first; although this section offers general information about these materials, you'll need specific instructions and plans to build walls from them.

Most suppliers sell stone by the ton or the cubic yard. To estimate the amount of stone you'll need, multiply the wall's length by its width, in feet. Multiply the result by the wall's width, also in feet. Divide by 27 to convert the number to cubic yards. Even if your supplier sells by the ton, s(he) will be able to give you an estimate based on your calculation. Turn to pages 64 and 65 for detailed instructions for building a mortared stone wall.

Brick

Even if it's only 2 or 3 feet high, a brick wall will lend an air of symmetry and formality to your backyard or garden. Brick is one of the easier wall materials to work with; unfortunately, it's also one of the more expensive, particularly if you use face bricks, the best choice for wall projects. They're uniform in shape, size, and color, and they're stronger and more attractive than building and concrete brick.

The amount of brick you'll need will depend on the size of brick you use; the length, height, and thickness of your wall; and the bond pattern you choose. The bond pattern, or the way in which the joints are staggered, will also affect the strength and appearance of your wall. Your local library will stock dozens of books that include plans and instructions for building brick walls.

Stone

Dry-stacked or mortared, stone walls have a natural, rustic charm perfect for the garden. Although they're usually more expensive and time-consuming to build, mortared walls can be less demanding than dry-stacked stone walls. You can use a variety of stone sizes and shapes in a mortared wall, even round and irregular river stones. For a dry-stacked wall, though, the stones must be very flat and more or less uniform in thickness. Fitting stones together in a dry-stacked wall can be a little like working a very heavy, three-dimensional jigsaw puzzle. In a mortared wall, you can use mortar to fill gaps where stones don't fit together well, and you can usually leave the stones' best faces exposed.

GARDEN BORDERS

Block

Block offers many of the same advantages as brick, and generally at a lower cost. It's available in a number of styles, colors, and shapes, and it's relatively easy to work with. It comes in standard sizes, so estimating quantities is a simple matter of multiplying the length of a wall by its width, then dividing by the size of the block. Of course, the least expensive, most-readily-available block—standard concrete—is also the least attractive. Fortunately, you can readily improve a concrete-block wall's appearance by coating it with mortar, a technique called rendering (see page 69).

Some suppliers carry reconstituted stone block, which is made from concrete, but has the texture and color of stone. Depending on where you live, you may also be able to find block made from adobe, clay, and glass.

Your local garden supply center will stock at least a few varieties of block, and they may be able to special order other styles. Follow the manufacturer's instructions for laying a block wall, or consult a book on the subject.

FOOTINGS

Regardless of the material you use, if you plan to mortar your wall, you must build it on a concrete footing. Otherwise, frost-heave will buckle, heave, and ultimately collapse it. (Dry-stacked walls are more flexible and can shift with the ground, so they don't require footings.) The directions here cover building a footing on a level site. Sloped sites require stepped footings, which are best left to professionals.

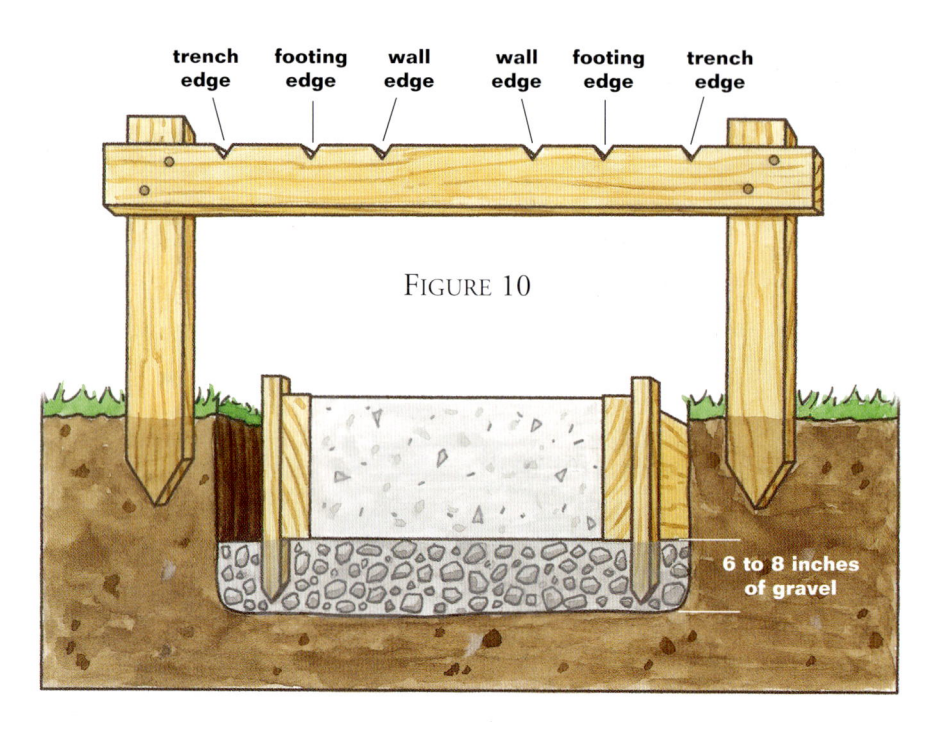

Footing Dimensions

In general, the footing should be twice the width of the wall, or two-thirds as wide as the wall's height—whichever is greater. Its trench should be 1 foot wider than the footing itself. The concrete for the footing should be as thick as the wall will be wide, and set below the frost line on a 6-inch bed of compacted gravel. If the frost line in your area is prohibitively deep, increase the amount of gravel to at least 8 inches, and set it above the frost line. (Otherwise, you might end up with more wall below ground than above.) Figure 10 shows a cross section of a typical footing. Check your local building codes before getting started, though; they may stipulate specific requirements for your area.

Constructing the Footing

Start by laying out the wall line: Use the technique described on page 54, making the batter-board crosspieces 1 foot wider than the footing's trench. Erect the batter boards so the center point of each crosspiece aligns with the planned center of the wall. Establish corners using the 3-4-5 method (see page 55).

Using figure 10 as a guide, measure along the crosspieces and notch where the edges of the wall, the footing, and the trench will be. Tie lengths of mason's twine between each set of batter boards at the trench-edge notches. Transfer the trench edges to the ground

FIGURE 10

trench edge · footing edge · wall edge · wall edge · footing edge · trench edge

6 to 8 inches of gravel

with inverted marking paint; then remove the twine lines.

If the trench needs to be deeper than 18 inches, longer than 30 feet, or if your site has particularly hard, rocky soil, consider renting a small backhoe to excavate it. Otherwise, dig the trench just as you would dig the base for a path (see pages 22 and 23), using the marking paint as a guide. Compact the soil with a hand-held tamper. Then add the gravel base and tamp it well.

Re-tie the lengths of mason's twine to the batter-board crosspieces, locating them in the notches indicating the footing's edges. Transfer these lines to the ground with inverted marking paint to indicate where to install form boards. (Form boards will hold the concrete in place as it sets; they're described in more detail on pages 24 and 25.) The form-board corners will be located exactly where the twine lines intersect; mark these points with rebar, as shown in figure 11.

Install the form boards as described on page 25, using 2x boards that extend the full depth of the footing, as shown in figure 11. Use a level to make sure the form boards along the outer and inner edges are even to one another. Hold the boards steady by nailing lengths of 1 x 4 lumber across them at 6-foot intervals, as shown in figure 11.

If you're building on unstable soil, you may want to reinforce the wall's footing. You can do this the same way you'd reinforce a concrete path base, as described on page 24.

If you're mixing your own concrete, a good recipe for wall footings is 1 part Portland cement, 2½ parts clean river sand, and—depending on its coarseness—1½ to 3 parts gravel. (The coarser the gravel, the more you'll need; consult your supplier for guidelines.) You can also use premixed bagged concrete, or have ready-to-pour concrete delivered to your site. If you're mixing your own or preparing bagged mix, consider renting a cement mixer for the day; otherwise, use a wheelbarrow and a hoe to mix it.

The concrete is the right consistency when it will hold distinct ridges; use the blade of a hoe or a shovel to test it. Then, starting at one end and working with at least one other person, pour the concrete. As one person pours, the other should spread the material evenly with a shovel. If your footing is fairly deep, pour the concrete in 6-inch layers. When you've finished pouring, screed the surface smooth with a scrap of lumber.

Allow the footing to cure for at least a week before building the wall. In the meantime, prevent cracking by sprinkling the concrete with water three or four times a day; keep it covered with plastic sheeting the rest of the time.

FIGURE 11

Building a Mortared Stone Wall

FIGURE 12

Building a mortared stone wall isn't complicated, but it is hard work and it will require more than just a weekend or two to complete. The end result, however, will last a lifetime. For a more rustic look, use natural stone (see pages 16 and 17); just be prepared to spend a little more time—and mortar—fitting the stones. For a more formal wall, use cut stone (see pages 15 and 16); although it's more expensive than natural stone, cut stone's uniform shape and size will make fitting the wall together go more smoothly.

MATERIALS AND TOOLS

- Tools and materials for trimming and cutting stone (see pages 110 through 112)
- Two 1 x 4 stakes
- Mason's twine
- Trowel
- Mason's jointing tool or a wooden stick
- Mortar (a mix of one part Portland cement to three parts sand to one-half part fireclay works well—see "Tips")
- Brick or concrete block (optional, see "Tips")
- Cut stone or natural stone (see "Tips")

TIPS

- If you're using cut stone and the face of the footing lies several inches below ground, bring the footing up to ground level by using concrete block as the first course; you'll save expensive stone. If you're working with natural stone, use your largest rocks for this first course.
- To find the best configuration—particularly if you're working with natural stone—dry-fit the stones before mortaring them in place.
- To estimate the amount of mortar, build a short section of wall, 4 or 5 feet long and to the desired height. Try to build the wall so that about one-fifth of its surface is mortar and four-fifths is stone. Extrapolate mortar quantities for the rest of the wall based on this sample section.

BUILDING A MORTARED STONE WALL 65

Instructions

1 Construct a concrete footing (see pages 62 and 63), and let it cure for at least a week.

2 Figure 13 shows the parts of a mortared stone wall. *Wythes* are vertical stacks, one stone wide. *Courses* are the wall's horizontal layers. *Bond stones* are long stones laid either parallel to the wall's face in a single wythe, or across the width of the wall, spanning wythes; they help tie the wall together and add to its stability. *Rubble* is small, irregularly shaped stone used to fill gaps between wythes. The *cap* seals the top course of the wall; it can consist of large, flat stones, or a 2-inch layer of mortar, slightly rounded to aid in water run off. Study figure 13; then sort your stones accordingly, setting them near the footing so they'll be close at hand.

3 Drive a stake into the ground at each end of the footing, a fraction of an inch from flush with where the face of the wall will be. Run mason's twine between the stakes to help keep each course in proper alignment.

4 For the corner bond stone, select a rock that's as wide as the wall. Spread a 2-inch layer of mortar along the first 3 or 4 feet at one end of the footing. Lay the corner bond stone in the mortar, and tap it with a rubber mallet to settle it. Repeat at the other end of the footing.

5 Work from the corner stones toward the middle, building both wythes at once. Spread the mortar in a ½-inch layer. Set stones with their flattest faces down. If heavier stones are squeezing too much mortar from the joint, use small wedges of wood to support them until the mortar stiffens; then remove the wood and pack the gaps with fresh mortar. Fill the space between stones in each wythe with mortar, and the space between the wythes with rubble and mortar shavings.

6 Before the mortar sets, rake out the face joints to a depth of about ½ inch with your mason's jointing tool or a wooden stick.

7 Raise the mason's twine, check for plumb with a level, and begin the second course, starting with the corner bond stones. Stagger the rocks in the second course over the first course in a "two over one, one over two" pattern, as shown in figure 12. Lay a bond stone every few feet for stability. When the course is complete, rake the joints.

8 Repeat until the wall is the desired height. Finish it by capping the final course with flat slabs of cut stone, or a 2- to 4-inch layer of mortar, rounded slightly.

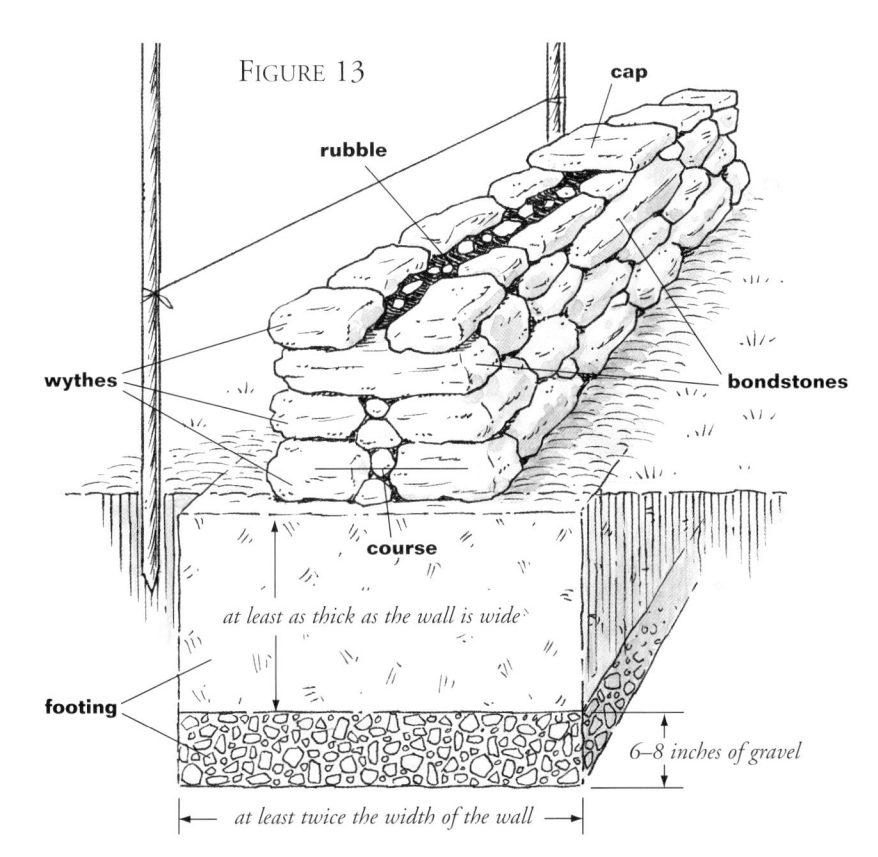

FIGURE 13
- cap
- rubble
- wythes
- bondstones
- course — at least as thick as the wall is wide
- footing
- 6–8 inches of gravel
- at least twice the width of the wall

Gates and Entryways

Gates and entryways are often treated as design afterthoughts, mentioned and installed only after the border itself. And yet the entry acts as the front door to whatever your hedge, fence, or wall surrounds. It's the one part of your border that people will actually use, touch, and really see. Thus it pays to plan and design gates and entryways thoroughly, and in conjunction with your border.

Start by deciding exactly where the entry or entries will be located, and how big they will be. Then choose a style based on both functionality and the impression you want your entry to give. Finally, build (or buy) and install the gate(s) and/or entryway(s), using the proper hardware and techniques.

LOCATION

Common sense and your site plan (see pages 46 and 47) should guide the placement of gates and entries. In general, they should be located where the border intersects traffic routes: the front walkway, garden paths, access to a garden shed, etc. If a gate will open directly off of a sidewalk, consider recessing it at least 3 feet from the walk; this will allow people to step off the sidewalk (and out of the way of passers-by) while opening the gate.

SIZE

To determine how wide an entry should be, consider who and what will be passing through it, and why. Allow 2 feet per person, and 1 foot for a piece of garden equipment. So a side entry to a service area should be at least 3 feet wide to allow for one person with a lawn mower to pass through comfortably; however, it's a good idea to measure your largest piece of lawn equipment to make sure it will fit through. Typically, a front entry should be at least 4 feet wide to accommodate two people walking side by side. Driveway gates need to be wide enough to accommodate the largest vehicle that might come through, but don't try to tackle a gate of this size on your own: Bring in professional help to design and install it.

An entry's height is a matter of both style and design. In general, though, most gates are about the same height, or just a little higher, than the surrounding border.

STYLE

From a simple break in a hedge to an ornate arbor draped in roses, styles of entries are as varied as the borders they open. The style you choose will depend on the border's style and function, the entry's location, and, of course, your personal taste.

Some entries, such as the front gate to your home, should stand out. For these, choose an entry style that contrasts with or differs at least slightly from the border. Visitors would easily be able to locate a wooden gate through a rock wall or an arched picket gate standing several inches higher than the surrounding picket fence.

Other entries, such as service accesses, should blend in almost seamlessly. In these situations, choose an entry style that mimics the border in every detail.

Even if an entry's style doesn't mimic the border, its function should. Borders built to ensure privacy and security or to contain pets should be equipped with entries that do the same. An open arbor through a high security fence would obviously defeat the fence's purpose; choose a high, solid gate instead, and equip it with a sturdy lock, if necessary.

DESIGN AND INSTALLATION

If you'd like to buy a pre-fabricated gate, arbor, or other entry, check with lawn and garden centers and landscaping suppliers. Unfortunately, you probably won't find a huge selection of styles; however, what you do find will generally include complete installation instructions and all the necessary hardware. If you decide to build your own entry, you'll find plans and instructions for literally hundreds of designs on the Internet and at your local library.

Whether you buy or build a gate or arbor, though, keep a few points in mind. First, gates and arbors should be sturdy without being too heavy. Weight is especially important for gates: They're attached on one side only, so that side must bear a heavier load. Choose a gate style that incorporates some kind of a brace to help spread the load evenly and to keep the gate from sagging on its hinges.

Remember that the posts to which a gate or arbor will attach should be set in concrete footings (see page 53). Check to make sure the posts are perfectly plumb and square to one another, and correct any deviation greater than ¼ inch.

To determine how wide the gate or arbor needs to be, measure the distance between the posts: Double check for plumb and square at this point by taking a measurement 6 inches from the bottoms of the posts and 6 inches from the tops. Then subtract between 1 and 1¼ inches to leave room for the hinges and the latch hardware.

For gates, choose the strongest, most weather-resistant hardware possible: Hinges should be very heavy so they'll be able to support the weight of the gate. Screws should be long enough to anchor the hinges securely in place without wiggling loose. There are a number of latch styles available, ranging from a simple hook-and-eye arrangement to bolt locks and other, more secure closures; pick a style that will provide the degree of security you want.

When you install a gate, be aware of the direction of its swing. In general, gates should open in, toward whatever the border is enclosing. The direction of your gate's swing, however, will depend on the features behind and in front of the gate, as well as on the site's slope. For instance, a gate at the top of a staircase should swing away from the steps, and a gate at the juncture of two perpendicular fence lines should swing against the corner, out of the way. A gate on a sloped site should swing downhill so its lower edge won't plow into the slope.

Enhancing Existing Borders

You and your family will probably move a few times before settling down in the house that will become your home. In the meantime, you may be faced with less-than-ideal hedges, fences, or walls installed or left in disrepair by the previous owner. Fortunately, sprucing up a garden border can be an inexpensive weekend project with great results.

PRUNING HEDGES

Transforming a shaggy hedge into a neat border costs little more than a pair of pruning shears and a few weekend hours. Before you start, though, consult a plant encyclopedia for guidelines regarding the best time of year and amount to prune the plants that comprise your hedge.

For informal hedges, thin out individual branches, while trying to maintain each plant's natural shape. For a wall-like effect, avoid pruning branches between neighboring plants.

Formal hedges should be pruned as one plant. The lower part of the hedge should be wider than the upper part to allow sunlight to reach all the branches, not just the ones at the top. Mark the desired top and bottom width of the hedge by driving four stakes into the ground at each end—two along each face. Tie a length of mason's twine between each set of stakes to guide your trimming.

LIVING DECORATIONS

If a fence or wall seems too stark or severe, you can soften its visual impact with vines, flowers, and other plants. Some vines, such as Boston ivy and Virginia creeper, naturally grasp onto surfaces by means of suction-cuplike adhesive disks; these plants can grow up solid masonry walls without trellises or special supports. Other vines, such as clematis and grape, have clinging tendrils that need to wrap around something to climb; they'll do well on chain-link fences, lattice screens, and other open-work borders. To encourage climbers that must be tied and trained, such as jasmine or climbing roses, install a trellis in front of the fence or wall; then gently tie the plant's branches to the lower rungs.

You can place potted plants on top of wider walls, or tuck cut flowers into niches or on shelves built in or on a wall or fence. If you don't mind inserting eye hooks and other fasteners into your border, you can hang potted plants directly on the face of a wall or fence. Finally, you can simply grow an attractive border of flowers along the bottom of a fence, wall, or hedge.

KNICKKNACKS AND TRINKETS

Indulge your whimsical side by decorating your garden border the same way you might embellish your indoor walls.

ENHANCING EXISTING BORDERS

Tuck your favorite weatherproof knick-knacks into the niches and protrusions in a stone wall. Add small shelves to brick walls or wooden fences, and use them to showcase interesting pieces of pottery. Display ceramic tiles against rendered walls. Just make sure your border ornaments will stand up to the rigors of outdoor life.

RENDERING

Rendering is the process of covering a wall with two or three coats of mortar. It's a relatively inexpensive way to turn a concrete-block wall into an attractive garden feature, or to transform the appearance of a brick wall. You can paint the top coat; add texture to it with a stiff broom; or embed it with sea shells, ceramic tile, or anything else that might look nice. Your library will have plenty of books with detailed instructions for rendering garden walls.

VENEERS

A veneer is simply a thin layer of one material bonded over another. Lightweight faux brick and stone are the most popular choices for outdoor walls. Applied correctly, a veneer can make an inexpensive concrete-block wall look like a stately border of solid brick or rock. You can purchase veneers at home and garden centers, and the manufacturer's information should include complete instructions for installation.

PAINT AND OTHER FINISHES

Painting is probably the most obvious way to change a border's looks. If you're painting a masonry wall, make sure it's completely clean, dry, and free of debris before you start. Although you can buy specially formulated masonry paints, any good-quality exterior paint should work well. Just be sure to apply a primer first.

Paint can do more than just improve a wooden fence's appearance; applied correctly, it will also extend your fence's life. Finishes formulated for outdoor use will protect wooden projects from decay, insects, sun damage, and the other dangers of garden living. For more information about wood finishes for outdoor use, see pages 115 through 116.

Be warned that painting and staining generally aren't among the easier ways to enhance a wooden fence, particularly if you have to remove an old paint job first. And if the old paint is chipping, you must strip or sand it off before applying a new finish. Some people actually recommend replacing the entire fence rather than stripping or sanding it, particularly if it's an open-work style. (Solid board fences are much easier to refinish because you'll only have to strip or sand and paint two major surfaces.)

Other wooden-fence treatments include bleaching and white washing. These treatments are appropriate for unpainted wood only, and are used for aesthetic purposes alone; neither offers anything in the way of protection or weather resistance. Bleaching is used to soften a too-new looking fence; basically, the application of a bleach-and-water solution causes wood to weather prematurely, actually speeding the deterioration of the fence. Bleach may make your fence look charmingly rustic, but it will also kill any vegetation it comes in contact with.

White washing involves applying a paste of lime, salt, water, and Portland cement. It will give your fence a pleasantly white, satiny finish, but like bleaching, it's not great for wood or for your garden.

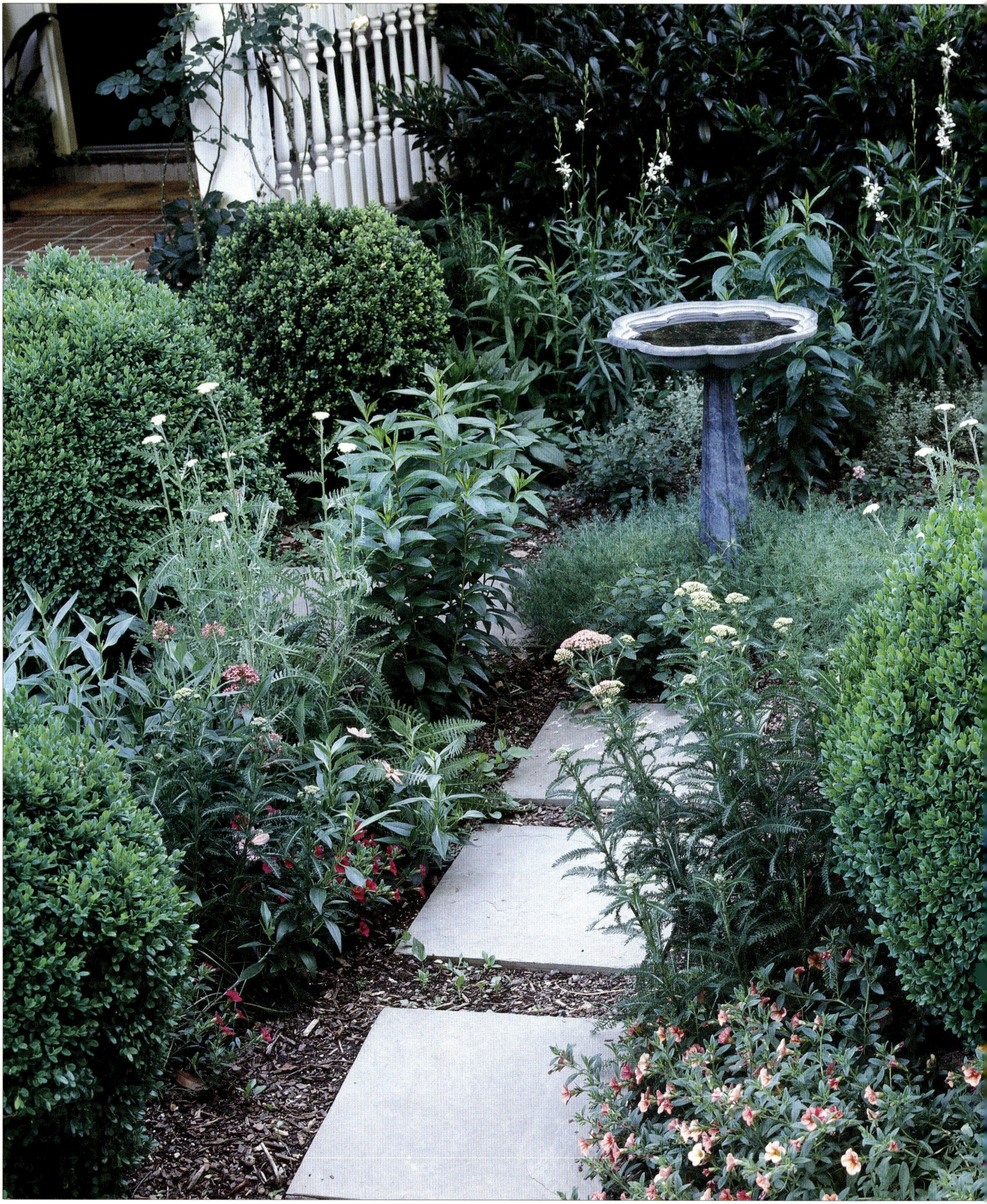

Garden Wildlife

As our daily lives grow ever more hectic, so, too, grows our need for refuge. After a day spent under the glare and buzz of fluorescent lighting, there is perhaps no refuge more welcoming than that provided by nature. When we witness the natural world, we reconnect with the fundamental elements of our own lives.

As this chapter will show you, when you invite wildlife to share your garden and backyard, access to that re-connection can be just a step or two away. Start by exploring ways to ensure harmony between your domestic friends and your feral guests. Then consider the kinds of wildlife you'd like to invite—and the kinds you should discourage—and learn how to do both. When you build a bat house, you'll get the best of both worlds: the company of the fascinating, nocturnal creatures whom the structure will beckon, and the rapid decrease in annoying insect life that will quickly ensue. Next, delve further into the worlds of some of the garden's most welcome visitors: butterflies and birds. Plant a butterfly garden, build a butterfly box, and use the art of mosaic to create a birdbath you and the birds will both love.

In fact, you may find that the projects and information in the pages that follow will tempt you as much as they tempt the resident wildlife. As you'll see, when you invite nature into your backyard, you do more than create a haven for wildlife: You create a refuge for yourself.

Domestic Harmony

Inviting wildlife to your backyard and garden is one of the easiest, most enjoyable ways to use your outdoor space. Before you start issuing invitations, though, consider those with whom you already share your part of the world: your family, your neighbors, and your pets.

YOUR FAMILY

Start by thinking of how you and your family currently use your outdoor space, and how you'd like to use it in the future. Do you hold frequent cook-outs and croquet matches? Do your kids use the backyard as an all-purpose play- and campground? If so, set aside a stretch of open lawn just for your family's activities; you'll be less likely to disturb your wild guests, and you'll still have space to enjoy yourselves.

Then consider the wildlife itself. Research the kinds of creatures you're likely to attract, and find out if any of them might be dangerous to children. Be sure to alert your kids to potential hazards. Show them pictures of poisonous snakes, insects, or spiders they might encounter; make it clear that these creatures play an important role in nature—but they can be dangerous to humans. Remind children that wild animals are just that: wild. They should be enjoyed, observed, and respected from a distance. Explain that nests and dens are off-limits, and that many animals and birds will desert their homes—and their young—if humans tamper with them. Educating yourself and your children will ensure everyone's safety: human and otherwise.

YOUR NEIGHBORS

Who wouldn't love to share their backyard and garden with adorable rabbits, flocks of perky birds, and the occasional inquisitive deer? The answer might be—your next-door neighbor. If you invite wildlife to your property, you're tacitly inviting it to the entire neighborhood; property lines are human constructs, and wild animals aren't likely to respect them. Talk with your neighbors about your plans, and find out if they have any concerns. If they do, try to work out a compromise. For instance, if you're planning an elaborate bird garden, and they're planning an exotic fruit orchard, you might volunteer to help protect their fruit from your birds by draping the trees in bird-proof netting during harvest season. And, of course, discuss fencing solutions that will help keep the wildlife in your yard from migrating to theirs. (See the chart on page 45 for garden border suggestions for various situations.) In this case, good fences may indeed make good neighbors.

YOUR PETS

Remember the animals that already reside on your property. Domestic pets play a crucial role in the success or failure of backyard wildlife havens. Dogs, especially puppies, will chase anything that moves. And while fuzzy puppies may be more or less harmless to most creatures, full-grown dogs are not. In fact, unleashed dogs are the leading predators of white-tailed deer.

Domestic canines aren't just on the giving end of potential danger, either. The temptation of a bounding rabbit can drag your dog all over the neighborhood—and right into traffic. To protect your dog and your wild guests, keep the former leashed or fenced in an area with plenty of food, water, and shade. (See page 45 for fence-height suggestions.) A leash, however, won't protect your dog (or your cat) from that rare wild animal infected with the rabies virus, so keep all of your pets' shots up to date. Ask your vet about other regional diseases that might pose a danger, and have your pets vaccinated against them, if possible.

As detrimental as dogs can be to wildlife, domestic cats are far worse. Every neighborhood in the country hosts what in nature would be an unnaturally high number of healthy, well-fed felines. And each one of these kitties has the natural instinct and ability to hunt and kill many of the guests you'd most like to visit your garden. Don't let your wildlife haven turn into a cat café! The best solution is to keep cats indoors at all times; for many people, though, this isn't practical. Try, at least, to keep cats in during the night. During the day, outfit your kitty in a bell-decorated collar. (Make sure the collar will automatically break or detach if it gets caught on something.) Theoretically, the bells will give potential prey fair warning of the cat's approach.

Consider using a cat repellant, too; these sprays and granules are usually quite effective. Simply follow the manufacturer's instructions to apply the repellent to the ground in areas where cats are not welcome. Finally, the same steps that will deter other garden predators will also work with cats (see page 76 and 77).

COYOTES: WANNABE SUBURBANITES

Until recently, the only time most people living in the eastern United States heard the high, lonely howl of the coyote was in movie theaters and during trips out West. These days, though, you're almost as likely to hear coyote yips in suburban Ohio as on the plains of west Texas.

As it turns out, the wily wild canine enjoys the same suburban lifestyle many Americans do. Strip malls and super highways may not constitute the coyote's ideal landscape, but our expansive yards and rolling parkways actually do approximate the wide open spaces of the animal's natural habitat. Another factor in the coyote's rapid expansion is the decimation of its primary predator, the gray wolf. Most importantly, however, the coyote is highly adaptable, and thrives with change.

Although coyotes dine on many creatures we consider pests, they should not be encouraged to visit the backyard. They're just as likely to prey on your cat as on the neighborhood rats, and they can be dangerous when frightened or hungry. Many of the same deterrents that keep other undesirable wild guests away will also work on coyotes (see pages 76 and 77). In particular, bring pets, their food, and garbage cans in at night. *Don't* feed coyotes, and if you find one that's injured, contact your local wildlife rehabilitator.

Attracting (and Deterring) Wildlife

When you hold an open house, some guests are more desirable than others; the same is true when you invite wildlife to your backyard. Be aware that strategies to woo the welcome will woo the unwelcome, too. This section does offer ways to discourage less-than-desirable guests, but keep in mind that no creature is inherently bad; each has a place and a purpose in nature, if not in your backyard.

GETTING FAMILIAR

As you probably know, to attract wildlife to your backyard, you must provide the basic necessities: food, water, and shelter. What form each necessity should take will depend on the type of wildlife you want and can reasonably expect. Get to know who might show up in your backyard and how they might behave. Ask your neighbors and local wildlife experts, and consult the Internet and your library. Then observe your surroundings over the course of a year and document who comes and when. If you know whom to expect and what they do (and don't) like, you'll be better prepared to attract (or deter) them. And, if you know a particular species never passes through your part of the country, you won't spend time trying to tailor a welcome mat for a guest who will never arrive.

An edge gradually blends one type of environment into another and attracts wildlife drawn to both types of habitat.

Fruit-bearing shrubs make excellent plantings for edges and provide food and cover for wildlife.

PROVIDING THE NECESSITIES

In general, though, the same kind of welcome mat will tempt a huge variety of creatures. And all you have to do to create it is this: Copy nature. Nature isn't tidy, so let your garden—at least a part of it—go wild. If they don't pose a danger, leave dead trees standing; dozens of creatures—from woodpeckers to chipmunks—will soon move in. Bats and butterflies love to roost behind loose tree bark, so don't strip it off. If you celebrate the winter

ATTRACTING (AND DETERRING) WILDLIFE   75

holidays with a cut tree, saw it into a manageable pile of brush after the festivities; then tuck it away in a corner of your garden to provide shelter for birds and other small animals. Let your flowers go to seed—literally; they're an excellent source of food for many birds and other granivorous (seed-eating) creatures.

If you'd like to take a more active roll, create *edges* throughout your property. An edge is where one kind of habitat meets another—where a forest borders a meadow, for example. Animals attracted to both types of habitats will show up at the edge. Your property already has several: the conjunction of lawn and flower bed, or of flower bed and shrubbery.

You can make existing edges more appealing by—you guessed it—copying nature. Nature isn't abrupt, so the transition from one edge to another shouldn't be, either: Plant low ground cover between lawn and flower beds, moving to taller, vertical plants closer to the beds. If your property borders a wooded area, merge the habitats with fruit-bearing shrubs such as blueberry or winterberry—hungry birds will come in droves.

The ideal edge would be a shallow pond transitioning into bog, then into "meadow"—or lawn. Build a small pond, and after a season, you'll probably have toads, frogs, turtles, bats, rabbits, and squirrels. If they're common to your area, you may also attract raccoons, opossums, coyotes, and deer—although the desirability of some of these guests is questionable (see page 76). If your pond is big enough, you may find water birds in there one day. Those water birds could have fish eggs stuck on their feet—and without any further effort on your part, fish might come to live in your backyard!

Don't worry if you don't have the space or inclination to build a backyard pond, though; even small water sources will attract plenty of wildlife.

Fill birdbath bowls or old garbage can lids with water, and place them on the ground in a shady spot where the water won't get too warm. (For more information about birdbaths, see pages 81 and 82.) Then just keep the bowls full—and clean.

Frequent cleaning should cut down on insects that might view your water source as an ideal breeding ground. Whatever you do, though, *don't* spray insecticides in your garden—not if you want wildlife. Instead, allow nature to take its course. Lady bugs will gobble up the aphids that want to gobble up your roses. And bats, birds, toads, frogs, and spiders—all high on the "welcome list"—will gobble up those annoying gnats and mosquitoes that want to gobble up *you*.

Bats are quiet, beneficial garden guests.

In fact, bats should be number one on most gardeners' welcome lists. They're quiet and clean and not at all deserving of their creepy reputation. Contrary to what popular culture would lead you to believe, bats just aren't interested in sucking your blood. Even vampire bats, which aren't found in North America anyway, prey on cows and chickens—not humans. What the average bat *does* prey on is insects—hundreds of them every hour, including Japanese beetles, gypsy moths, flying ants, and mosquitoes.

If you live in the United States, southern Canada, or northern Mexico, you should be able to tempt at least one species of bat to your backyard. Water and plenty of insect life will bring them in; well-placed shelter will convince them to stay. The bat house project on pages 78 and 79 will make a cozy home for your backyard bats.

Another airborne, nocturnal creature high on most people's welcome list is the flying squirrel. No, they won't de-bug your lawn, pollinate your plants, or perform any other garden service; what they will do is keep you highly entertained. Flying squirrels don't actually fly, but rather glide from tree to tree by means of loose, furry flaps of skin that extend from the forelegs to the ankles of the hind legs. They also dance, stomp, and frolic; hug and kiss each other; and seem to enjoy human company, too. In short, they pretty much out-cute all other backyard wildlife.

If you live in the southern or northeastern United States, California, or southern Canada, and your property is endowed with deciduous hardwoods (such as hickory, oak, or maple), you're probably hosting flying squirrels already—whether you've seen them or not. You're even more likely to have them if you have a bird-friendly backyard (see pages 80 through 82); flying squirrels, like their non-gliding kin, enjoy many of the same foods that birds do. You won't see flying squirrels during daylight hours, though, so to enjoy their antics, install dim lighting near your bird feeders. Then, from dusk on, check the feeders every hour or so. If they show up at 9:30 one night, it's a good bet they'll be back around 9:30 the next evening.

DETERRING WILDLIFE

If you've attracted flying squirrels, you've probably drawn their diurnal relatives, too. Tree squirrels are cute, inventive, and acrobatic; they're also voracious and destructive, cleaning out bird feeders and flower beds alike. Some people love them, some people tolerate them, and some people *hate* them. If you're among the last group, you do have a few options for discouraging squirrels. First, if you want to feed the birds but not the squirrels, buy or construct feeders that are squirrel-proof; the most common variations are covered in wire mesh that

ATTRACTING (AND DETERRING) WILDLIFE

birds can fit through but that squirrels cannot. Install all mounted bird feeders on smooth poles well away from tree branches, rooftops, and anything else from which a squirrel could leap. Make the smooth poles even less climbable by mounting inverted wastebaskets or cones of barbed wire on them, or by coating them in a thick layer of slippery grease. Install rings of sheet metal (with the edges filed completely smooth) around the openings of nesting boxes (see page 82) to prevent squirrels and other predators from widening them.

The same deterrents that prevent squirrels from feasting at your bird feeders will also help keep raccoons from dining on your song birds' eggs. Although some people have made pets of raccoons, these little masked bandits should be discouraged from visiting your backyard: They will destroy your garden. *Don't* feed them! If you do, they'll come to expect hand-outs and they'll perform all kinds of mischief to get them. Raccoons love your garbage, so discourage nightly thefts by keeping trash cans inside at night. Bring pet food indoors during the evening, too. Otherwise, you're providing easy pickings for squirrels, raccoons, opossums and—undesirable on anyone's list—rats.

Deer are magnificent but very destructive garden visitors.

In fact, rats may be the only clear-cut choice for the not-welcome list. Most other creatures have their human champions who will always be happy to see them. Furry, cute, and harmless to everything but your greenery, rabbits definitely fall into this category. If you're more fond of your vegetables than of visiting bunnies, protect the former by fencing garden areas with 1-inch-mesh chicken wire, at least 24 inches high, and buried 4 inches underground. For added protection, staple strips of 1 x 2 lumber along the edge of the buried portion.

You'll need slightly higher and sturdier barriers to dissuade your garden's other number-one enemy—deer. Without a doubt, there's something awesome about viewing a 150-pound deer from your kitchen window. And with the nationwide decline in deers' predators (wolves and mountain lions), it's a sight becoming more and more common all around the country. It's also a sight that will grow old quickly. The magnificent creatures will decimate your shrubbery, your flowers, your vegetables, and anything else green and growing they can fit in their mouths. Once deer discover your tasty garden, keeping them out is very difficult. Fencing offers the best solution, although hungry deer will jump fences 6 feet—and higher. What they generally won't jump, however, are barriers they can't see *beyond*; deer don't like to leap if they can't see a safe landing zone, so buffering even a low fence with a thick boundary of shrubbery may stop them.

If you really want to feed deer (or other wildlife that's not always welcome in the backyard), consider this neighbor- and garden-friendly option: Go to an area at least ¼ mile from the nearest home or garden and leave your offering of fruit, ear corn, or fresh vegetation such as alfalfa there. Don't leave hay, though; it doesn't provide the nutrition deer require.

Building a Bat House

Inviting bats into your backyard is a handy way of dealing with a host of pesky insects. These voracious nocturnal creatures will do a better job of ridding pests than those expensive "bug zappers" do. And all you need to welcome your guests is a bat house, built from wood and hung from a tree or on the side of your house.

MATERIALS AND TOOLS

- 24 linear feet 1 x 6 cedar, rough on one side
- ¾-inch-thick scrap wood blocks
- 34 #8 x 1½" deck screws
- 34 6d (2") galvanized box nails (optional)
- Tape measure
- Circular saw with rip guide or table saw
- Power drill with #8 pilot bit and #8 countersink
- #2 Phillips driver tip or Phillips-head screwdriver
- Router with ¼" roundover bit with ball bearing (optional)
- 150-grit sandpaper

TIPS

- All the interior surfaces of the house should have a rough texture oriented horizontally. This provides a good foothold for the bats to roost. You can substitute exterior rough siding if you wish, or you can score smooth boards with the tip of a screwdriver.
- Simplify assembly by pre-boring all the joints for screws. (See page 97.)
- Soften any sharp edges on the boards to make the house more comfortable for its inhabitants. You can round sharp edges by hand with 150-grit sandpaper, or use a router equipped with a ¼" roundover bit.

Instructions

1 Cut all the parts (A through E) to the dimensions in the cutting list. Crosscut a 15° miter at one end of each side (A) with a circular saw or on the table saw using a miter gauge. Be sure to match the sides, making mirror images of them, so each rough side is oriented inside the house. On the table saw or with the circular saw, rip 15° bevels on the back edge of the roof (E), the top edge of one front piece (B), and the top edge of one baffle (D).

BUILDING A BAT HOUSE

2 Drill and countersink the screw holes in the sides (A), back (C), and roof (E). Drill two rows of holes in each side, locating the holes ⅜ inch and 1⅞ inches from the front edge for each respective row. Start the first hole in each row by measuring 3¾ inches up from the bottom of the side. Drill a second countersunk hole 4 inches above the first hole. Continue up 1½ inches for the third hole, and repeat the drilling sequence from there for a total of eight holes per row, or 16 holes per side. Use the same procedure to lay out and drill the holes in the five back pieces, except for the uppermost back piece. For the top piece, locate the holes ¾ inches and 3 inches up from its bottom edge. Then drill a hole through each end of the top (E), centering each hole widthwise and ⅞ inch in from the end.

3 Now assemble the pieces. Begin by screwing the five back pieces (C) to the sides (A), starting at the bottom and working your way up the sides, board by board. Make sure the ends of the back boards are flush and square to the sides as you screw them fast.

4 Add the four baffle pieces (D) between the sides (A), screwing through the sides, into the ends of each baffle. Start from the top and work down, attaching the top baffle with its beveled top edge even with the miters on the sides. Use ¾-inch-thick scrap blocks between the back and the baffles to help position them.

5 Attach the front boards (B), slipping them between the sides (A) as before and screwing through the sides and into their ends. Start from the top, with the first beveled board flush with the miters on the sides, and work towards the bottom.

6 Add the roof (E), screwing it to the top ends of the sides.

7 Finish by drilling a small hole through the center of the back at the top for a screw or nail. To keep your guests happy, hang the bat house at least 20 feet off the ground, in a draft free spot.

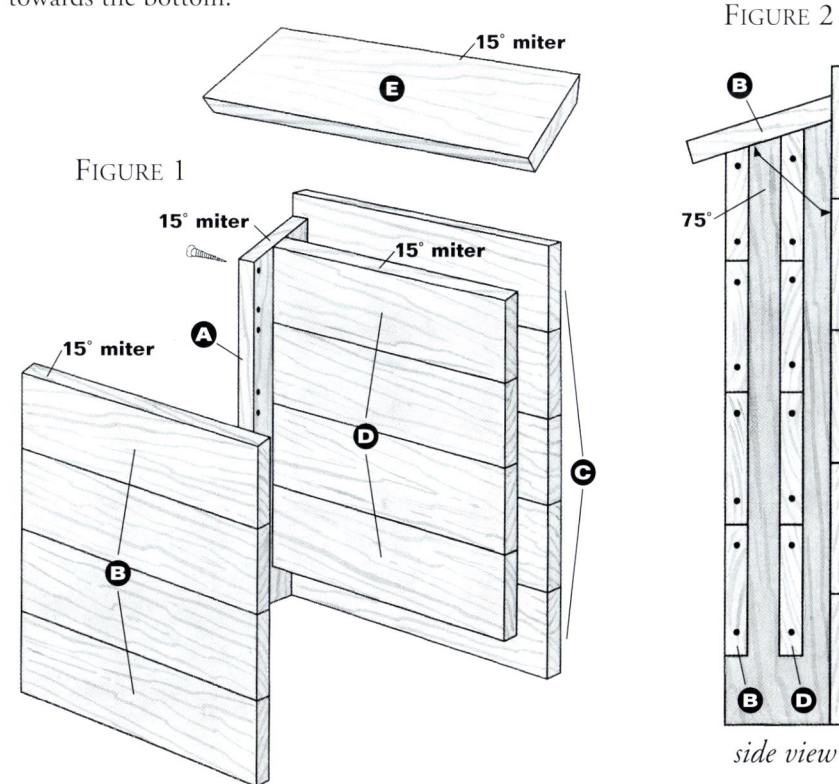

CUTTING LIST

CODE	DESCRIPTION	QTY.	MATERIAL	DIMENSIONS
A	Sides	2	1 x 6	3" x 25¾" to long point of 15° miter
B	Front	4	1 x 6	14" long
C	Back	5	1 x 6	15½" long
D	Baffle	4	1 x 6	14" long
E	Roof	1	1 x 6	16½" long

FIGURE 1

FIGURE 2

side view

Inviting Birds

The danger of attracting a yard full of birds is that once they arrive, you may have a hard time tearing yourself away from your bird-viewing perch. You'll come to know each species that visits, and within each species, the distinct personalities of individual birds. You'll compete with your neighbors to see who can lure more; and you'll be delighted when—each year—the migrators show up right on schedule, like (organic) clockwork. Without a doubt, birds are fascinating. Fortunately for us, they're easy to attract, too!

THINK VERTICAL

As with any form of wildlife, to attract birds, you must provide the basics: food, water, and shelter. What's different about birds is that they inhabit a vertical, as well as a horizontal, plane. In North America alone, there are over 2,000 species of birds—each with its favorite height at which to dine, drink, and roost (sleep). Research which species are likely to visit your backyard and what will attract them; then, as you read the rest of this section, think vertical.

FOOD

Food will bring in flocks of birds. Keep your avian friends happy and healthy by providing them year-round variety. Start by planting with birds in mind: Choose fruiting shrubs, such as blueberry, blackberry, bayberry, and wax myrtle, which will all provide cover, as well as food. Fill your flower beds with black-eyed Susans, forget-me-nots, purple coneflowers, poppies, snapdragons, and sunflowers; deadhead some of them to bring back blooms for the butterflies, but let plenty more go to seed to produce tasty pickings for birds. Native grasses, such as June grass, sea oats, Indian grass, and switchgrass also produce tasty seeds. Consult a local nursery for other bird-friendly shrubs, flowers, and grasses that will do well in your area.

Left to seed, forget-me-nots will provide food for backyard birds.

During the summer, a well-stocked garden and the surrounding natural landscape will provide plenty of food. Even so, birds always appreciate extras. From autumn through spring, the extras you offer may be essential. A caution before you start setting out seed and suet, though: Feeding wild birds encourages them to stay in your backyard, rather than seek out natural sources of food—they will come to depend on you, so be prepared to keep feeding them through the entire lean season.

Your local home and garden center will stock dozens of kinds of food for wild birds. To choose what to buy, know for whom you're buying. Suet (hard, rendered animal fat) will attract insect-eaters. Seeds will, of course, attract seed-eaters. And sugar-water solutions will attract nectar-eaters, such as hummingbirds. Like humans, many birds are omnivorous and will eat a variety of food. Birds that particularly enjoy suet include woodpeckers, chickadees, bluebirds, mockingbirds, warblers, kinglets, titmice, nuthatches, jays, robins, starlings, and wrens. The chart to the right lists a few popular backyard birds and the seeds they prefer.

Just as there are dozens of kinds of feed available, there are dozens of ways to present it to birds. Again, know whom you're feeding—and think vertical. Some birds prefer to peck seed off the ground, so scatter some in the lawn for them (well away from brush, where predators can lie in wait). Others require suspended feeders. Hummingbirds are attracted to red, so choose a red feeder, but don't dye its contents! Use a ratio of 1 part sugar to 4 parts water, and leave it clear.

Regardless of how you feed birds, keep the feeding area clean. Seed can mildew and rot, and birds will get sick if they eat it. Rake up seed on the ground every few days, and clean out feeders with a mild bleach-water solution (use a ratio of 1 part bleach to 10 parts water) at least once a month. Clean hummingbird feeders every three days. And don't serve suet during the summer; it will go rancid in the heat.

WATER

Birds love taking baths, and you'll love watching as they flap and splash and kick. Put out a proper birdbath, keep it full and clean, and the birds will find it.

You can make a birdbath out of just about any water-bearing container with the appropriate dimensions. Birds like to feel the bottom under their feet, so the bath should be very shallow along the edges, sloping gradually to no more than 3 inches deep at its center. It should be wide enough for birds to really splash and flap around in. And its rim should be slightly rough and wide enough for birds' feet to grip.

If you really want to draw a flock, install a small fountain or waterfall. Birds are attracted to the sound of running water, and they love to play under it.

Common Backyard Birds and Their Favorite Seeds

BIRD	PREFERRED FOOD
Mourning doves	Black-oil sunflower seeds, white and red proso millet
Blue jays	Hulled peanuts, seeds of all types
Chickadees	Black-oil and striped sunflower seeds, hulled peanuts
Nuthatches	Striped sunflower seeds and black-oil sunflower seeds
Native sparrows	White and red proso millet
Red-winged blackbirds	White and red proso millet
Common grackles	Striped and hulled sunflower seeds, cracked corn
Cardinals	Sunflower seeds of all types
Grosbeaks	Sunflower seeds of all types, cracked corn, safflower seeds
House finches	Black-oil and striped sunflower seeds, niger seeds
Dark-eyed juncoes	White and red proso millet, fine cracked corn
Goldfinch	Niger thistle seed, hulled black-oil sunflower seeds

Note: Seed should be fresh and of good quality, or birds may turn up their beaks at it. Consider offering a tray of grit (sand or canary grit, for instance), too; birds store it in their gizzards to help grind seeds.

GARDEN WILDLIFE

Choose the location of your water feature carefully. Place it about 10 feet from overhanging branches—close enough that birds can flee to cover, but too far for predators to jump from. And consider installing at least two—one on the ground and one on a pedestal—to satisfy birds most comfortable at each location. Think of how changing seasons will affect the bath, too; for instance, water might get too hot in sunny spots during the summer, but freeze more quickly in the shade during winter. (Inexpensive birdbath water heaters are available at most places that sell other bird supplies.) Finally, place water features well away from feeding sites; soggy seed will soil the water. Birds hate dirty water as much as we do—and it can make them sick. So rinse water features every few days, and schedule a scrubbing with the same bleach-water solution you'd use on feeders (see above) once every two weeks.

SHELTER

Even for short-term summer visits, birds need shelter from predators and the weather. If you want birds to winter or raise their families in your backyard, you'll need to provide cold-weather shelter, too.

To go *au naturel,* use plants and natural objects. Most shrubs that provide food (see page 80) also offer excellent cover. The ideal backyard for birds would include both deciduous and evergreen trees, too. Piles of wood (situated away from your home and other wooden structures so they won't attract termites) also offer good nesting sites. If you can offer all these types of natural cover, you'll have provided for birds all along the vertical axis, from ground-level bramble to penthouse branches.

About 50 common species of birds will also enjoy human-made shelter, or bird houses (often called nesting boxes). All of these species are "cavity dwellers"—birds that build their nests in the hollows of trees or other cavities. (No matter how nice your nesting box, you'll never tempt a tree-dweller, such as the Baltimore Oriole, to take up residence in it.) Woodpeckers, titmice, wrens, and bluebirds are all cavity dwellers. Each species has specific preferences regarding doorway dimensions and nesting height, so be sure to check what your guests like before you build (or buy) and install birdhouses. (Most birding books include this information.) Avoid birdhouses with perches, though; only predatory birds use them—to prey on the song birds inside. Check the suggestions on pages 76 and 77 for keeping other predators out of nesting boxes and feeders.

Woodpeckers, natural cavity dwellers, will nest in dead trees and in human-made shelters.

AND YOU

As you create your backyard bird haven, remember why you're doing it. Of course you like providing for wildlife and doing your part to help nature. But let's face it, you also want to enjoy the birds! And that means being able to see them. Place at least some of your bird feeders, houses, and baths in your line of sight, and all of them in locations where you'll be able to fill and clean them easily—in summer and winter. Pick up a bird identification guide and a pair of binoculars; both will help you get to know your guests even better.

Decorating a Purchased Birdbath with Mosaic

This bright and original birdbath is fun to look at even when the birds aren't around. If you live in a cold climate, cover and invert the top for the winter and enjoy the pedestal as a reminder of the spring to come. See the previous page for tips on siting your birdbath.

MATERIALS AND TOOLS

- Concrete pedestal-style birdbath with removable top
- 15 to 20 ceramic plates and saucers in solid colors and assorted designs
- Small figurines (optional)
- Safety glasses
- Tile nippers (see "Tips" below)
- Small containers for sorting mosaic pieces
- Fine-tip permanent marker
- Mortar (a good mix for mosaic projects is one part Portland cement, two parts sand, and one part water)
- Mixing container for mortar
- 2 bricks or heavy stones
- Notched trowel
- Gray-sanded grout
- Mixing container for grout
- Grout spreader or polyethylene foam wrap
- Palette knife
- Sponge
- Lint-free rags
- Commercial concrete sealant (optional)

TIPS

- Tile nippers are hand-held tools designed to cut ceramic objects into square, round, and irregular shapes. You can find them at any craft-supply store. To use tile nippers, simply place the jaws so that they overlap the edge of the piece to be cut by about 1/8 inch; then squeeze the handles firmly and evenly.
- Look for inexpensive ceramic plates at garage sales and thrift stores.
- Freezing water can cause both mosaic and concrete to crack; protect the birdbath top from moisture during the winter by turning it upside down and covering it with plastic sheeting. The mosaic portion stands upright and will shed moisture, so it should weather well as long as it's grouted properly (see step 9).

Instructions

1 Don your safety glasses for this step. To prepare mosaic pieces, start by breaking the plates in half with your tile nippers. Remove the rims from the plates, and trim the rim pieces into roughly rectangular pieces, 1 to 1½ inches wide; you'll use these pieces on curved portions of the project. Break the flat portions of the plates into 1- to 2-inch pieces that are fairly uniform in thickness; you'll use these pieces on flatter surfaces. Discard the raised "feet" of the plates and any other pieces that are thicker than the rest; then sort the remaining pieces into sorting containers according to color and size.

2 If you're using figurines in your design, trim them to fit flush against the pedestal. You may be able to set them directly on the pedestal, or you may need to use tile nippers to break off parts. Be careful, though: three-dimensional figurines can easily shatter into several unusable pieces.

3 Determine which part of the pedestal that you want to cover with mosaic pieces. (The flatter areas are the easiest to work on; sharply curving areas require much smaller mosaic pieces.) If you have a design in mind, sketch it on the pedestal with a pencil or marker.

4 Mix the mortar in a small container.

5 The pedestal will be easier to work on if you place it horizontally, so lay the pedestal on its side and prop it with the bricks or heavy rocks to keep it from rolling.

6 With the notched trowel, spread the mortar on a small section of the pedestal. Set the mosaic pieces in the mortar, following your pattern, if you're using one. Use the tip of the palette knife to remove any excess mortar that may have squeezed up between the tiles. Spread additional mortar and set mosaic tiles to finish the section. Allow the section to dry overnight before turning the pedestal to work on another portion.

7 Three-dimensional objects and figurines need to be set in mortar and allowed to dry overnight before turning the pedestal. If the object doesn't fit flush with the pedestal, apply more mortar to its back before setting it in place.

8 After you've finished the final portion of the pedestal, allow the mosaic to dry overnight before grouting.

9 Mix the gray-sanded grout according to the manufacturer's instructions. Then use the grout spreader or the polyethylene foam wrap to spread the grout over the surface of the mosaic. Use pressure to force the grout into all the spaces between the mosaic pieces. Allow the grout to set for about 15 minutes; then remove the excess grout with the polyethylene foam wrap or with rags. Follow the manufacturer's recommendations on the grout packaging to remove any grout "haze" that develops.

10 Allow the mosaic to cure according to the grout's package directions before placing the birdbath in your garden.

11 If desired, you can use a commercially available sealant for concrete to protect your birdbath. Follow the manufacturer's instructions for application.

Inviting Butterflies

Regardless of how beneficial or hardworking, no other insects are as universally welcome in the backyard and garden as butterflies. Not only are they lovely to look at, they're also super-efficient pollinators. And if you keep your garden well-stocked with butterflies and their younger incarnations, caterpillars, you're likely to draw plenty of song birds, too; the latter enjoy many of the same plants and flowers, as well as the butterflies and caterpillars themselves.

THE BUTTERFLY LIFE CYCLE

You're probably familiar with the butterfly's complicated life cycle, but it's a story that bears repeating: An adult butterfly lays eggs on host plants. The eggs hatch into caterpillars, which feed on the host plants, non-stop. After growing larger and larger and molting several skins, each caterpillar becomes a chrysalis, cocooned in a pupal case. Inside the pupal case, the chrysalis transforms into an adult butterfly—a process that can take as little as a week or as long as a year, depending on the species. When the transformation is complete, the pupal case splits open and the butterfly emerges. It pumps its wings full of fluid, lets them dry, then flies away—hopefully, somewhere within your garden!

PROVIDING FOR BUTTERFLIES AND CATERPILLARS

The point of re-telling the butterfly life cycle is this: Butterflies and caterpillars have different needs. Butterflies sip nectar from brightly colored flowers, while caterpillars gnaw their way through copious amounts of host-plant leaves. (Yes, if you want butterflies, be prepared to have some ragged, caterpillar-eaten plants in your garden.) To attract the greatest number of butterflies, cater to the creatures at each stage of their lives. The butterfly garden plan that starts on the following page goes a long way toward doing this. Don't worry if the climate in your area isn't right for some of the plants shown; as long as a flower is brightly colored and will grow in a sunny spot, chances are your local butterflies will like it. For alternate host plants, consider parsley, fennel, and hop tree, all favorites of—among others—the black swallowtail's caterpillar.

In addition to nectar, adult butterflies also sip water, but only from very shallow sources. The best way to provide butterflies with moisture is to splash some water on the ground, creating damp spots and small mud puddles. And even this step won't be necessary in areas that receive plenty of rainfall.

What butterfly lovers in wet climates *will* need to offer their guests is shelter. At night and during inclement weather, butterflies sneak into cracks and crevices. The butterfly box project on pages 88 and 89 will provide temporary shelter for short-lived summer butterflies. It can also serve as a nesting box for any of the 40-some species of longer-lived butterflies that hibernate.

Finally, remember that butterflies are, indeed, insects. If you want them in your garden, don't use pesticides!

A Butterfly Garden Plan

The plan illustrated here is designed around a stone walkway, and includes birdbaths to accommodate visiting avians (just splash a little water out on to the ground for the butterflies), and a bench-arbor for human visitors. Like the creatures they beckon, plants that butterflies love enjoy full sun, so plant your butterfly garden in an open area that's sheltered from gusty winds. Most of these plants do best in well-drained soil, and should be watered regularly. Keep flowers blooming—and butterflies coming back—all season by deadheading (removing flower heads as the blossoms fade).

A HYACINTH BEAN
Lablab syn. Dolichos

Minimum temperature: 45°F

Herbaceous, perennial twining vine, also grown as an annual. A favorite host plant for many varieties of caterpillars. Fast-growing from seed. Height to 10 feet. Feasting caterpillars will leave the plant looking ragged, so you may want to tuck it somewhere inconspicuous.

A BUTTERFLY GARDEN PLAN

B BUTTERFLY BUSH
Buddleja syn. Buddleia

Zones 6–9, depending on species

The mainstay of any butterfly garden. Genus of about 100 fast-growing evergreen, semievergreen, and deciduous shrubs. *B. davidii, B. alternifolia, B. crispa,* and *B.* 'Lochinch' are particularly attractive to butterflies. Small tubular flowers come in a variety of colors, including lilac, blue, orange, pink, and white. Bloom from midsummer through first frost. Height to 12 feet. Prune to 1 foot each year for luxuriant growth.

C LANTANA
Verbenacea

Zones 8–12

Fast-growing shrubs. Evergreen and deciduous varieties available. Will bloom all year in frost-free areas. Available with yellow, orange, pink, and purple flowers, as well as "confetti" mixes. Crushed foliage has pungent odor that some people find unpleasant, but that butterflies love. Fruit is poisonous—don't plant in gardens that will be visited by children. Height from 2 to 8 feet. Prune hard in spring. Feed and water very lightly.

D STAR CLUSTERS
Pentas lanceolata

Minimum temperature: 45°F

Tough, heat-loving shrub. Year-round-blooming perennial in tropical areas, annual in areas that experience frost. Star-shaped flowers come in muted shades of red, white, pink, blue, and lavender. Good for mass-plantings. Slow to flower—buy plants already in bloom. Height to 4 feet. Feed monthly during summer.

E PINKS
Dianthus

Zones 3–9, depending on species

Low, mounding ground cover. Evergreen perennial, also biennials and annuals. Blooms late spring through early summer. Dainty, miniature carnation flowers. Over 300 species available, most with pink blooms which are the most fragrant. Also in white, shades of red, yellow, and orange. Heat and drought tolerant. Deadhead all at once with shears, leaving a grey, moss-like mat. Will remain a soft grey in winter.

F ASTERS
Aster

Zones 3–10, depending on species

Annuals, biennials, perennials, and subshrubs. Blooms late summer to early fall. About 250 species, with heights varying from ground cover to 6 feet. Petals of many colors: white, red, pink, blue, lavender, or purple, usually with yellow centers.

G ZINNIAS
Zinnia

Minimum temperature: 50°F, depending on species

Herbaceous perennials and annuals. Blooms June to October. Height varies from 8 inches to 3 feet. Wide color range in white, and shades of red, yellow, orange, and lavender. Easy to grow, very inexpensive. Sow from seed. Love hot weather, so sow them last. Group en masse and use to fill in spaces between other plants. No need to deadhead.

H CONEFLOWER
Echinacea

Zones 3–9, depending on species

Robust, heat-loving, herbaceous perennial. Blooms in late spring through autumn. Height varies from 8 inches to 5 feet. Daisy-like blooms in purple, pink, and white. Deadhead for continuous bloom. Good cut flowers.

I CONEFLOWER
Rudbeckia

Zones 3–9, depending on species

Tough, easy-to-grow, herbaceous annuals, biennials, and perennials. About 20 species, including black-eyed Susan. Blooms summer to midautumn. Orange and yellow daisy-like flowers. Good cut flowers; cutting encourages reblooming later in season.

Building a Butterfly Box

Butterflies are fair-weather creatures. During the night and on rainy days, they seek out cracks and crevices where they can rest until the sun comes out again. Mounted near plants butterflies love (see pages 86 and 87), this sleek box will provide a safe haven for some of summer's most welcome guests.

MATERIALS AND TOOLS

- 14 linear feet 1 x 6 cedar
- 2 linear feet 1 x 8 cedar
- 8 3d (1¼") finish nails
- 17 #8 x 1¼" deck screws
- Power drill with #8 countersink and #8 pilot bit
- #2 Phillips driver bit or Phillips-head screwdriver
- Small square
- 8" quick clamps or bar clamps
- Circular saw
- Miter saw (optional)
- Router with ¼" roundover bit with ball bearing (optional)
- Exterior wood glue
- 150-grit sandpaper

TIPS

- This project is made from red cedar; see page 117 for other decay-resistant woods.
- Simplify assembly by pre-boring all the joints for screws. (See page 97.)
- Before assembling the house, round over all the exposed edges by hand with 150-grit sandpaper, or use a router equipped with a ¼" roundover bit.

Instructions

1. Cut all the parts (A through J) to the dimensions in the cutting list. Leave the ends of the sides (E) and fronts (G) square for now.

2. Clamp and glue a thin spacer (B) to each thick spacer (C), keeping the edges flush.

3. When the glue has dried, glue and clamp a spacer assembly to each face of the divider (A), 1 inch from the top of the divider and centered on its width. (See figure 3.)

4. Center the divider (A) over the floor (D), with its edges overhanging the floor by 1¼ inches on each side. Use a single screw through the floor to attach it to the bottom of the divider.

5. Using the circular saw or a miter saw, cut a 45° miter on each of the four sides (E) as shown in figure 3.

6. Position a mitered side (E) over the edge of a door (F), aligning the top of the door flush with the lower corner of the miter. Drive a screw through the side, into the edge of the door, locating the screw 1¼ inch down from the top of the door, as shown in figure 3. Screw another side to the opposite edge of the door the same way. The door should swivel easily between the sides; loosen the screws, if necessary. Repeat the procedure with the remaining sides and door.

BUILDING A BUTTERFLY BOX   89

7 Place a side-door assembly with the inside of the door (F) against one end of the floor (D), and the sides (E) fitted around one spacer assembly at the top. The back edge of the sides should be flush with the back of the thicker spacer (C). Drive a screw through each side, into the floor; then hammer a finish nail through each side, into the thick spacer. Securing the side-door assembly this way should leave a ½-inch gap between back edge of the sides and the divider (A). Attach the second side-door assembly the same way.

8 Cut two 45° miters in the top of each front (G), making sure the resulting angle is 90° and the point at the top is centered on the stock. (See figure 3.)

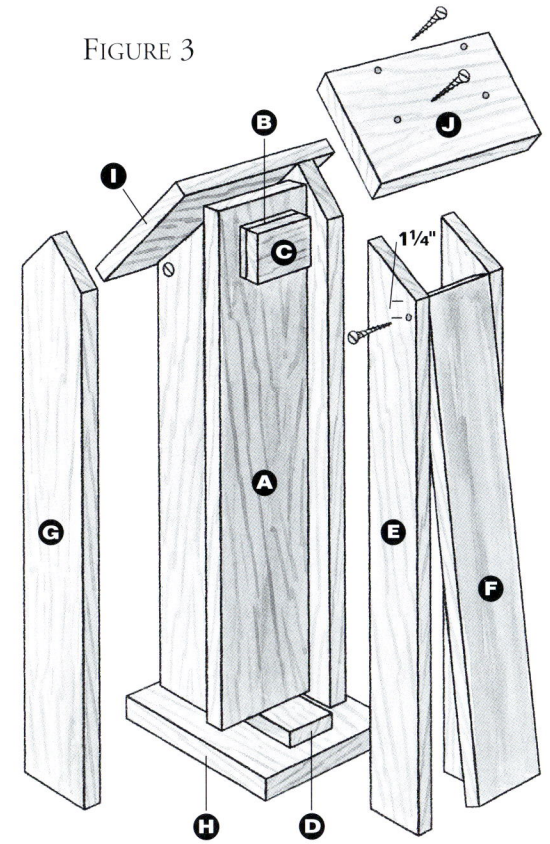

FIGURE 3

9 Glue the mitered fronts (G) to the divider (A). Center each front on the edge of the divider, with its bottom edge flush with the sides (E).

Spread a bead of glue on the edge of the divider. Use quick clamps to secure the parts until the glue dries.

10 Center the bottom (H) over the side-door assemblies, then drive two screws through the bottom, into the floor (D).

11 Center the narrow roof (I) over the top of the butterfly house, with its top edge flush with the miters on the fronts (G) and overhanging each side (E) by 2¼ inches. Attach the roof with two screws driven through the roof, into the ends of the sides.

12 Finally, add the wide roof (J). Align the ends of the narrow and wide roofs (I and J), with the top edge of the wide roof flush with the face of the narrow roof. Drive two screws through the face of the wide roof, into the edge of the narrow roof. Then add two more screws, driving them through the wide roof, into the ends of the sides (E).

CUTTING LIST

CODE	DESCRIPTION	QTY.	MATERIAL	DIMENSIONS
A	Divider	1	1 x 6	5½" x 21¾"
B	Thin spacers	2	½" scrap	2¼" x 3"
C	Thick spacers	2	1 x 6	2¼" x 3"
D	Floor	1	1 x 6	5¼" x 3"
E	Sides	4	1 x 6	2½" x 22" from long point of miter
F	Doors	2	1 x 6	3" x 19¼"
G	Fronts	2	1 x 6	2¼" x 23" from tip of miter
H	Bottom	1	1 x 8	7½" x 7½"
I	Narrow roof	1	1 x 6	5¼" x 9"
J	Wide roof	1	1 x 8	6" x 9"

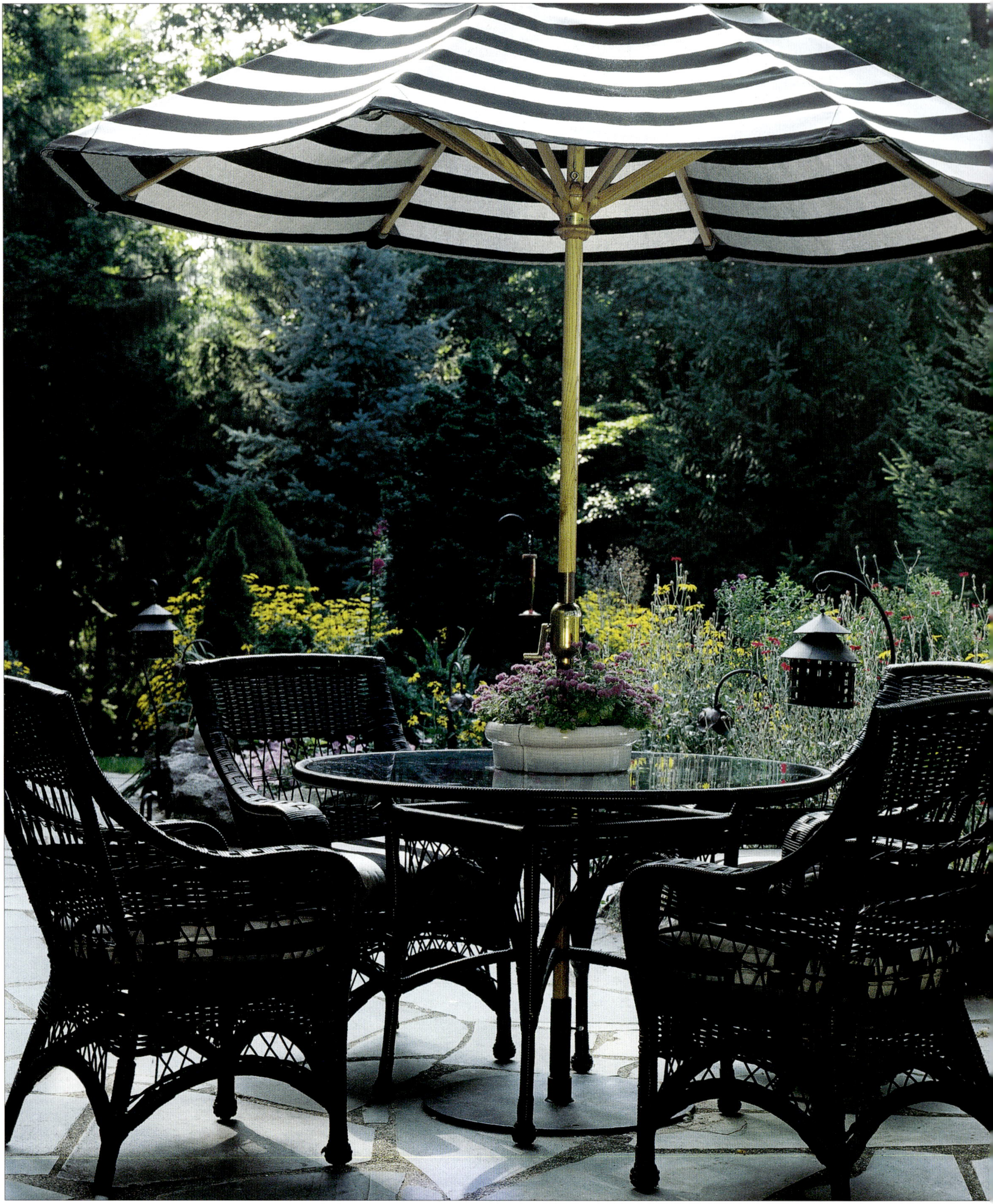

Garden Furniture

Maintaining our outdoor space can be a labor of love—weeding the vegetable patch, planting bulbs in the flower beds, even mowing the grass. Too often, though, labor is *all* we do in our lawn and garden. We forget that we care for our outdoor space so we can *enjoy* it. Play in it. Dine in it. *Relax* in it.

If you're not taking full advantage of your tract of nature, maybe it just isn't inviting enough for *you*. It may boast feeders for every bird that could conceivably stop in your neighborhood—but lack a picnic table where your family can enjoy Sunday brunch! This chapter is about finding that picnic table—and benches to match. It's about selecting a chair that will lure you outside for an afternoon with a great book and a glass of iced tea. It's about furnishing your outdoor "rooms" so they're just as comfortable as any room indoors.

Start by assessing your needs—and your space. Then read about different types of furniture material—how much they cost, how well they'll stand up to life in your backyard, and how to maintain them. Learn strategies for successful furniture shopping, and review tips for building your own furniture. Finally, dive into some projects. Build a patio, an outdoor table and matching chair, and an Adirondack-style love seat. All are easy enough to build that you'll still have plenty of time for what's really important—enjoying your backyard and garden.

Selecting Outdoor Furniture

Whether you're buying or building, you may be surprised by the wide variety of outdoor furniture that's available. To choose the best furniture for your needs, start by considering how—exactly—you plan to use it. Then think about the space where you'll put it. Finally, your budget, your climate, and your personal taste will help you determine the best kind of furniture material for your needs.

FUNCTION

It may seem obvious, but the first step toward furnishing your backyard and garden is one that many people neglect: Imagine the details of how you and your family want to use your outdoor space. For instance, do you plan to dine outdoors? Then you'll need a table and seating. (See pages 104 through 109 for instructions for building an outdoor table and matching chair.) If you imagine yourself relaxing in the shade while you read the Sunday paper, you'll probably want a lounge chair, a hammock, or a recliner of some sort. (See pages 100 through 103 for instructions for building a Adirondack-style love seat that's perfect for a day of lounging.)

Be sure to balance your fantasies with reality. Are you really going to cook outdoors every summer weekend, or is that your spouse's fantasy for you? The answer could mean the difference between a full-fledged cooking set-up (complete with a rolling food cart and buffet) and a small bistro table where the delivery person can leave the pepperoni with extra cheese.

SPACE

You don't need much room to enjoy outdoor furniture—even a small patio or patch of level ground will do. (The project on pages 98 through 99 will show you how to build a simple patio without a lot of fuss or money.) As you're deciding where you want to locate your furniture, take note of shady and sunny spots; you may want to take advantage of—or avoid—these places. If you don't have any natural shade, consider adding an umbrella or an awning to your furniture wish-list. Then take measurements of the space(s) you choose so you'll have an idea of what will fit as you consider which pieces to buy or build.

Just like indoor furniture, outdoor furniture should be appropriate to its setting. The key is to match the size and style of your furniture to the space available. Massive Adirondack chairs are perfect for larger lawns and porches, but they might overpower a tiny balcony. Likewise, a wrought-iron suite would look great on a slate- or

SELECTING OUTDOOR FURNITURE

gravel-floored patio, but it would be unwieldy and unsafe on the grass of an open lawn. Rustic furniture will complement a backyard planted to attract wildlife (see chapter 3), but it would look out of place in a formal garden.

MATERIALS

Today's outdoor furniture is made of everything from gorgeous, weather-resistant redwood to environmentally friendly recycled milk jugs. The material you choose will depend on the climate in your area, your budget, and, of course, what you like.

Wood

In general, outdoor wooden furniture tends to have clean, simple lines—think classic picnic tables and stately fret-backed benches. Perhaps because it's a natural material, wood seems to fit any kind of garden setting. You can leave wooden furniture unfinished for a more natural appearance (most wood will weather to a silvery grey), or finish it with paint, stain, or varnish to create a more polished look.

The cost of wooden furniture varies widely, mainly with the type of tree it's made from. Furniture made of weather-resistant wood such as teak, redwood, and cedar generally costs more. The extra money will buy you many more years of low-maintenance enjoyment because these kinds of wood will hold up well to the weather, even without a protective finish. Furniture made from non-weather resistant wood such as pine can be just as beautiful as that made from more expensive wood; however, it will rot quickly if you don't finish it with paint or stain that contains an anti-fungal agent and an ultra-violet protectant. Most finishes will need to be touched up or reapplied ever year or so. Finished or unfinished, keep your wooden furniture looking its best by washing it at least once a year with a soft sponge and a mild solution of soap and warm water; then rinse and dry it.

Avoid placing wooden furniture in direct contact with the ground; even weather-resistant wood or well-finished pieces will eventually succumb to rot. If you want to place wooden furniture right out in the lawn, nail glides made from high-density plastic to the feet of chairs and tables (most hardware stores carry these furniture glides).

Wicker

Traditional wicker furniture is woven from natural materials such as willow, rattan, cane, rush, and raffia. Today, wicker-style furniture is also available made from (or sometimes coated with) weather-resistant resin (see the following page). Whether made from natural fibers or resin, wicker furniture usually has either a Victorian or Oriental look. This reflects the flexible material's popularity during the 19th

True wicker will fare best in a shady spot.

century, when it was used to create the intricate designs popular at that time.

Wicker furniture made from or coated with resin can be used in any outdoor setting, and should be cared for in the same manner as other resin furniture (see below). Traditional wicker, however, will fare better on shady patios and in sun rooms where harsh sunlight won't dry it out.

To care for real wicker, wet it thoroughly once a year using warm water and a sponge; this will replenish the moisture in its fibers. Wicker should also be cleaned on a yearly basis. Start by vacuuming it; then sponge it off with a mild solution of soap and water, and rinse it clean. Remove tough dirt in cracks and crevices by scrubbing gently with a toothbrush. If the furniture has mildewed, wash it with a solution of one part bleach to five parts warm water; then rinse it with water. (This treatment can lighten wicker, so be sure to apply the bleach-water solution evenly to the entire piece.) Use lemon-oil furniture polish to restore the appearance of unfinished wicker.

Plastic Resin

The least expensive of outdoor furniture materials, plastic resin can also be one of the most durable. High-quality resin will resist fading and cracking, and, of course, it won't rot—even if you leave it sitting in the mud all spring. (Cheaper resin may fade when exposed to too much sunlight.) Furniture made of plastic resin is available in almost every shape and style imaginable, from flimsy discount pieces to sturdy, tasteful Adirondack chairs.

Most plastic furniture is easy to move from place to place and to store. (Many pieces break down or fold up for easy storage.) As with most things, the more money you're willing to spend, the better quality you'll get. Do consider buying furniture made from recycled plastic; not only will you get well-made pieces, you'll also help create demand for products made from recycled materials—good for you and for the environment.

Caring for plastic resin furniture couldn't be easier. Simply sponge it down with warm, soapy water when you notice it looking a little dingy. Then rinse it clean and dry it with a soft cloth.

Metal

Metal furniture runs the price gamut, ranging from very moderate in cost to very expensive. The most common metals for outdoor furniture are aluminum and cast-iron, with the former generally being much less expensive than the latter.

Aluminum furniture tends to have a very contemporary look, perfect for city patios and urban lofts. Thanks to the material's light weight, furniture made from aluminum is easy to move from one spot to another. Although it will resist rust, aluminum furniture is vulnerable to dings and scratches. When you purchase aluminum furniture, look for pieces with a baked-on or enamel finish; these will stand up to minor surface damage better than bare aluminum. Keep the finish looking good by washing and waxing the pieces three or four times a year. (Use commercial car wax, following the manufacturer's instructions.) You can revive damaged aluminum by buffing it smooth with a No. 00 steel wool pad moistened with paint thinner.

Wrought-iron furniture requires far less maintenance than aluminum, but usually carries a higher price tag. It's available in a range of styles, from simple contemporary pieces to intricate Victorian designs. Wrought iron should retain its good looks for years with very little effort on your part. Simply check the pieces for chipped finish; if you find spots of exposed metal, touch them up with a rust-resistant primer.

Concrete and Stone

If you want outdoor furniture that will stand the test of time, and you're very sure you'll want it to remain in the same place year after year, *and* you don't mind spending a fair chunk of money, concrete or stone may be a good choice for you. Both materials look *permanent*. They can also look formal or casual, depending on the particular style. Concrete furniture is readily available, whereas you may have to bring in a stone mason to custom-build stone furniture—a service that will require more than a few extra dollars in your garden-furnishing budget.

Maintaining concrete or stone furniture involves little more than rinsing it off when it looks dirty.

BACKYARD BARGAINS

Yard sales and flea markets can be great sources for garden furniture. Here are a few tips to help you get the best deals:

■ Ask the seller about the cost, brand name, and history of each piece. Counter his or her sales pitch by asking, "Why are you selling it?" The question is so direct it may elicit a more straightforward answer than you'd otherwise receive.

■ Test used furniture as thoroughly as you'd test new pieces (see page 97): Sit in chairs, lean on tables, and check that racks and planters sit firmly on the ground. If a piece wobbles, its joints are probably loose; if all a loose joint's parts are intact, you can often repair it easily with water-resistant glue and a few clamps.

■ Check the hardware. Is it frozen? Rusted? Frozen screws and nails are difficult to remove without damaging wood, but rusted hardware can usually be removed and replaced easily.

■ Pay special attention to the bottom of wooden furniture where it comes in contact with the ground. If the wood is soft and "punky," the piece is beginning to rot. Don't buy it!

■ Look for cracks in wooden furniture, and remember—they'll only get bigger.

■ Inspect the finish. If it's a film-type finish, such as paint or varnish, and it's peeling, you'll have extensive stripping and refinishing to do. Stains and other penetrating finishes, on the other hand, can be sanded and re-coated easily.

■ Even if a rusty bench or peeling chair isn't useable as furniture, it might make a great planter or garden accessory.

Buying Garden Furniture

We tend to buy outdoor furniture on impulse, based on a great sale or a sudden desire to lounge in the sun on the first warm day of spring. As a result, we often end up with garden furniture that's just not quite right—maybe it doesn't fit in with the rest of the garden, or perhaps it's simply not comfortable enough. Fortunately, if you shop for outdoor furniture with the same focus and intent you'd use to buy indoor furniture, you're sure to create a garden "room" that's as relaxing and inviting as any on the other side of the walls.

Test outdoor furniture before buying it—kick off your shoes and read a chapter of a book to make sure a piece will be comfortable.

TIPS FOR BUYING FURNITURE

- To get the best furniture for your needs, you should see, touch, and use the pieces before buying them. If you find something you love online or in a catalog, contact the retailer to see if they have an outlet near your home. Otherwise, try to find a similar style of furniture nearby for "testing" purposes.
- Dress the part. Wear the same kind of comfortable clothing you'd normally wear to relax. If you wear shorts and a tee-shirt to read the Sunday paper, wear shorts and a tee-shirt on your shopping trip.
- Test all the pieces that seem to fit your general needs, not paying attention to particular styles or cost at this point. If you're looking for a picnic table and benches, sit on the benches to make sure they're the correct height relative to the table. Lounge in the lounge chairs. Rock in the rocking chairs.
- As you're testing the furniture, consider the other people who might use it. If you often host elderly company, pay attention to how easy or difficult it is to sit down in and rise out of seating.
- Check for stability and sturdiness, as well as for comfort. Do the tables and chairs sit evenly on the ground, or do they wobble? Note the pieces that feel good and that are structurally sound; mark the others off your list.
- Examine the remaining furniture with an eye to practicality. Will it fit your space? Your budget? Your lifestyle? A gleaming white outdoor sofa may look great in the showroom, but how well will it stand up to kids and life under an oak tree full of birds? Narrow the list again.
- At this point, you should have a small collection of furniture that's comfortable, within your budget, and practical for your needs. From this group, make your final selection, choosing the pieces that are the most durable and, of course, appealing. Then write the check and await delivery, iced tea in hand.

Building Wooden Garden Furniture

When you build your own wooden outdoor furniture, you'll be able to create durable pieces you love, gain the satisfaction of "doing it yourself," and save money, too! All you need to get started are good plans, a few basic tools, and some free time.

PLANS

This chapter includes plans for a graceful Adirondack love seat (pages 100 through 103), a great-looking outdoor table and matching chair (pages 104 through 109), and handy portable patio squares (pages 98 through 99). For additional plans, check your local library, the Internet, and woodworking and tool catalogs. Make sure the plans include a picture of the finished product (so you'll know what you're getting into), and detailed illustrations.

TOOLS AND WORK AREA

If you own or can borrow or rent the following tools, you should be well-equipped to build most outdoor furniture: a circular saw with a rip guide; a jigsaw; a hand or power miter saw; a power drill with drill bits and driver bits (you can substitute hand-held screwdrivers for the driver bits); a hammer; an assortment of C-clamps, bar clamps, and quick clamps; and layout tools such as a measuring tape, straight edge, and square. A router with assorted bits is also handy to have for rounding edges and for making a variety of decorative profiles. (Alternately, you can smooth edges by hand with sand paper wrapped around a sanding block, or with a block plane.)

You'll also need a work area with good lighting and ventilation, proper electrical outlets, and a sturdy work bench. Your work bench can be as simple as a piece of ¾-inch-thick plywood glued or clamped to a couple of saw horses. Just make sure it's stable and that the surface is at a comfortable working height.

TIME

Most projects will take longer to build than you think. Base your time estimate on the complexity of the project, your experience, and your tools. Then double the number of hours you think you'll need!

A FEW MORE TIPS

- Build with weather-resistant wood (see page 117), or plan to apply and maintain an anti-fungal, weather-resistant finish that will also provide protection against ultra-violet rays.
- You can increase the weather resistance of unfinished wood by raising its grain, then sanding it smooth. Here's how: Thoroughly soak the surface of the completed furniture using water and a sponge. Place the furniture outside and let it dry completely. Then cut back and smooth the raised grain with sandpaper.
- Use weather-resistant nails, screws, and other hardware. Appropriate treatments and materials include the following, listed from least to most expensive (and effective): galvanized steel, aluminum, epoxy-coated, stainless steel, and bronze.
- As for all wooden projects, you can make assembly easier by pre-boring the joints for screws to prevent splitting. At all screw locations, use the countersink bit to allow the screw heads to sit flush to the surface, then position the parts to be joined and drill a pilot hole through the countersunk hole in the first piece and into the second piece.
- Use moisture-resistant woodworking glue specifically labeled for outdoor use. Look for Type II glue or for the new polyurethane glues.
- Wooden furniture shouldn't be allowed to sit in puddles—even shallow ones. However, if you live in a climate where this is unavoidable, protect your furniture by nailing glides made from high-density plastic (available at any hardware store) to the bottoms of table and chair legs, and to any other piece where it comes in contact with the ground.

GARDEN FURNITURE

Building a Portable Deck

If you've always wanted an outdoor deck, but wanted to avoid the hassle of building a permanent structure, this portable deck is the answer. Built from individual squares that fit together, you can arrange, rearrange, or move the squares as you like. You can even take the deck with you if you move to a new location!

MATERIALS AND TOOLS
(for one deck square)

- 35 linear feet 5/4 x 6 pressure-treated pine decking
- 22 linear feet 2 x 6 pressure-treated pine
- 3 linear feet 4 x 4 pressure-treated pine
- 48 #8 x 2½-inch galvanized, coarse-thread wood screws
- 34 16d (3½ inch) galvanized, ring-shank nails
- Hammer
- Power drill with #8 countersink and #8 pilot bit
- Phillips driver bit or Phillips-head screwdriver
- Power miter saw or circular saw

CHOOSING THE RIGHT PATH   99

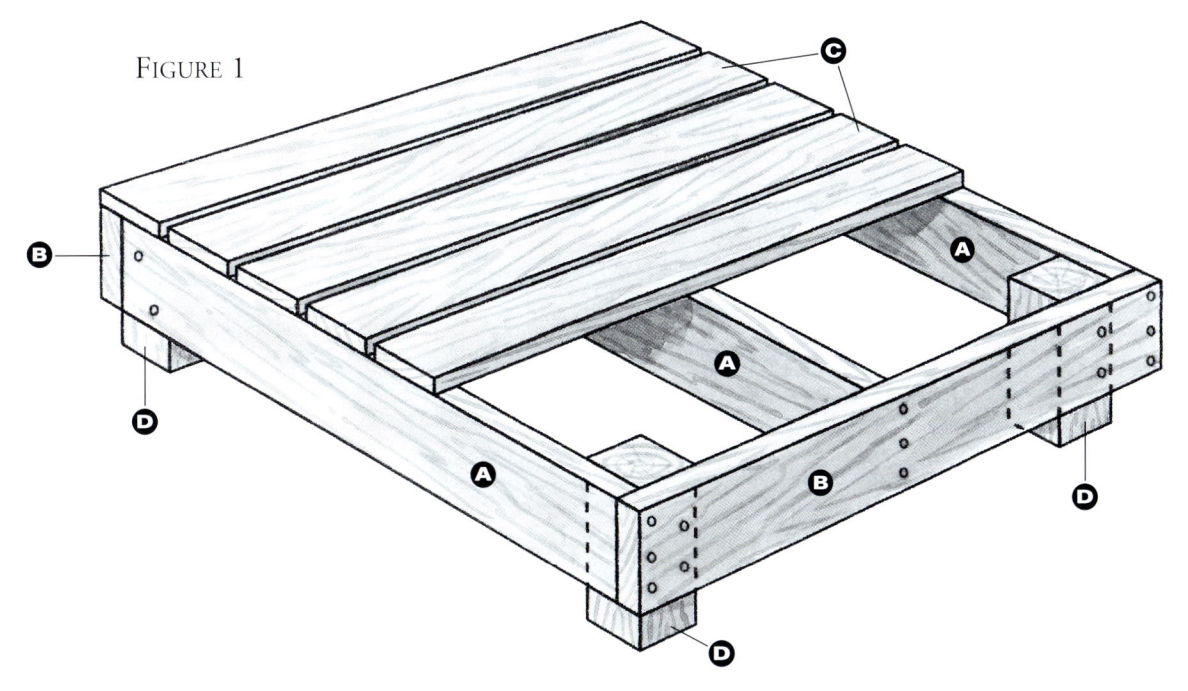

FIGURE 1

Instructions

1 Cut the short and long joists (A and B) to the lengths noted in the cutting list.

2 Position two of the short joists (A) on the floor, parallel to each other and roughly 43 inches apart. Place the two long joists (B) over the ends of the short joists, as shown in figure 1. At each of the four corners of the frame, nail through the long joist, into the ends of the short joist, using three nails spaced evenly across the joint.

3 Add the third short joist (A) to the frame, as shown in figure 1. Secure the joist as before, nailing through the long joists (B), into the ends of the short joist.

CUTTING LIST (for one deck square)

CODE	DESCRIPTION	QTY.	MATERIAL	DIMENSIONS
A	Short joists	3	2 x 6	43" long
B	Long joists	2	2 x 6	46" long
C	Deck boards	8	5/4 x 6	46" long
D	Legs	4	4 x 4	7½" long

4 Crosscut the eight deck boards (C) to length. Position them over the assembled frame, perpendicular to the short sides, as shown in figure 1. Make sure the two outer boards are flush to the outside of the frame; then space the remaining six boards about ¼ inch apart between the outside boards. Countersink and drill pilot holes through the deck boards, and secure them to them to the frame by driving two screws per joist.

5 Crosscut the four legs (D) to length; then turn the assembled frame assembly over so the decking is on the bottom. Position the legs in each corner. Attach each leg by driving nails through each outside corner and into the leg, using two nails through each short and long joist (A and B).

6 Turn the completed deck over, and paint, stain or seal it with a couple coats of water sealer, following the manufacturer's directions.

Building an Adirondack Love Seat

Longer than a traditional Adirondack chair, this outdoor sofa is perfect for sharing with a friend or for stretching out all by yourself. Like conventional Adirondacks, the seat and back slope to a comfortable angle for long hours of relaxed repose.

MATERIALS AND TOOLS

- 8 linear feet 1 x 2 pine
- 29 linear feet 1 x 4 pine
- 45 linear feet 1 x 6 pine
- 5 linear feet 2 x 4 pine
- 36 #8 x 1¼" deck screws
- 80 #8 x 1½" deck screws
- 4 stainless-steel carriage bolts, ⅜" x 2" with nuts and washers
- 2 stainless-steel carriage bolts, ⅜" x 2½" with nuts and washers
- Power drill with #8 countersink and #8 pilot bit; ⅜" drill bit
- #2 Phillips driver bit or Phillips-head screwdriver
- C-clamps
- Small square
- Jigsaw
- Circular saw with rip guide
- Miter saw (optional)
- Table saw (optional)
- Scrap blocks of wood
- Scrap stick, ⅛" thick x 50" long
- 150-grit sandpaper

TIPS

- The bench shown is made from yellow pine finished with a clear wood sealer. See page 117 for alternative, decay-resistant woods.
- Simplify assembly by pre-boring all the joints for screws. (See page 97.)

BUILDING AN ADIRONDACK LOVE SEAT

Instructions

CUTTING LIST

CODE	DESCRIPTION	QTY.	MATERIAL	DIMENSIONS
A	Back legs	3	1 x 6	39" long
B	Seat rail	1	1 x 6	46" long
C	Front legs	2	1 x 4	24" long
D	Seat slats	6	1 x 4	46" long
E	Back slats	8	1 x 6	32" long
F	Back rails	2	1 x 2	46" long
G	Arms	2	1 x 6	27" long
H	Arm rail	1	2 x 4	52" long
I	Arm supports	2	1 x 4	9" long

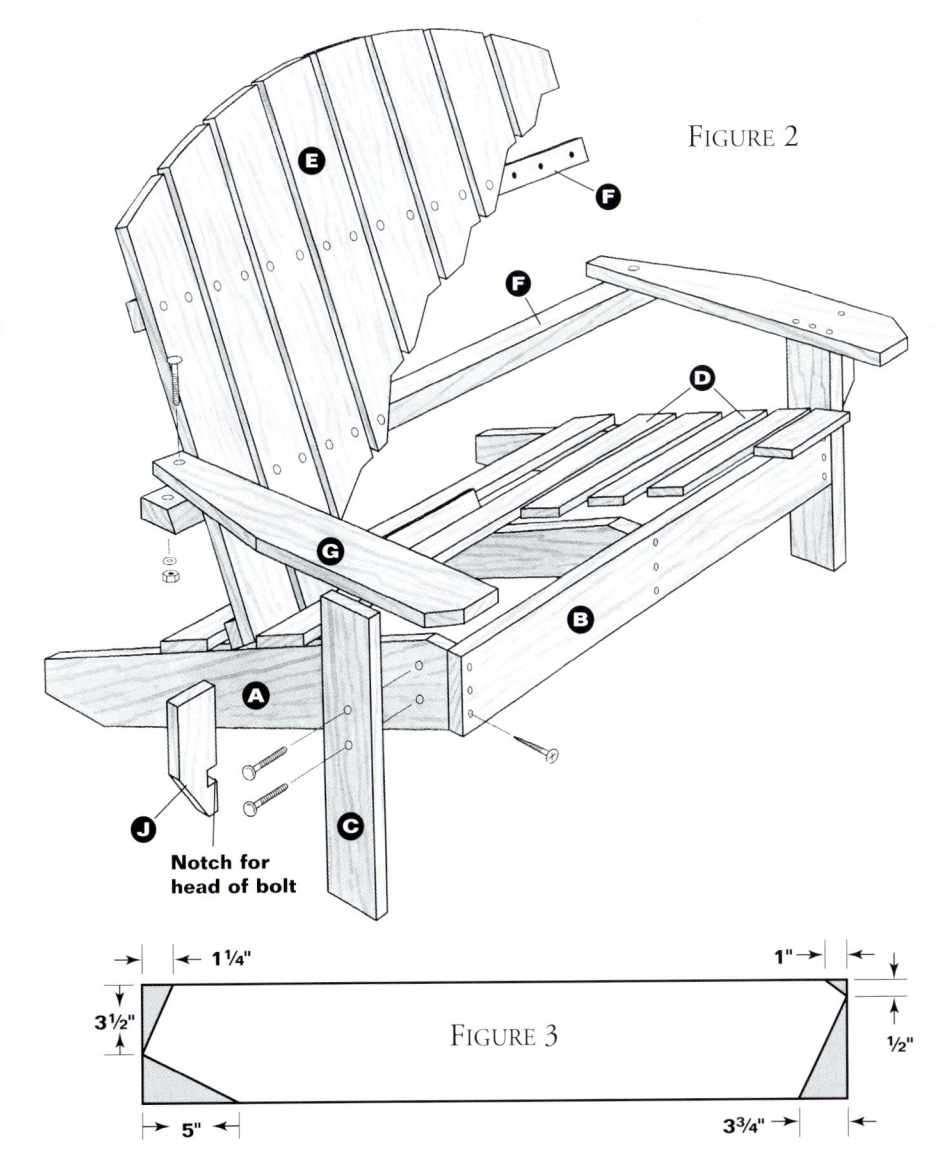

1 Cut all the parts to the dimensions shown in the cutting list. Leave the back legs (A), back slats (E), arms (G), arm rail (H), and arm supports (I) square for now. You'll cut the angles on these parts later.

2 Mark the three back legs as shown in figure 3. Draw straight lines between the measurement points; then saw on the waste side of your lines with the circular saw or a miter saw.

3 Working on the floor or on a large assembly table and using figure 2 as a guide, join the back legs (A) to the seat rail (B), using three 1½-inch screws per joint. You'll find it easiest to assemble the parts with the frame upside down. Align the two outer legs flush to the ends of the rail and even with its top edge, and position the middle leg in the center of the rail.

4 Turn the seat assembly right-side up, and add the front legs (C). Position each front leg such that the top of the seat assembly is 18 inches above the bottom of the leg, as shown in figure 4 on the next page. Temporarily clamp the parts together, then drive two 1¼-inch screws through the inside of the back leg, into the front leg. Remove the clamps; then strengthen the joints by drilling two ⅜-inch holes

FIGURE 2

Notch for head of bolt

FIGURE 3

3½"   1¼"   1"   ½"   5"   3¾"

FIGURE 4

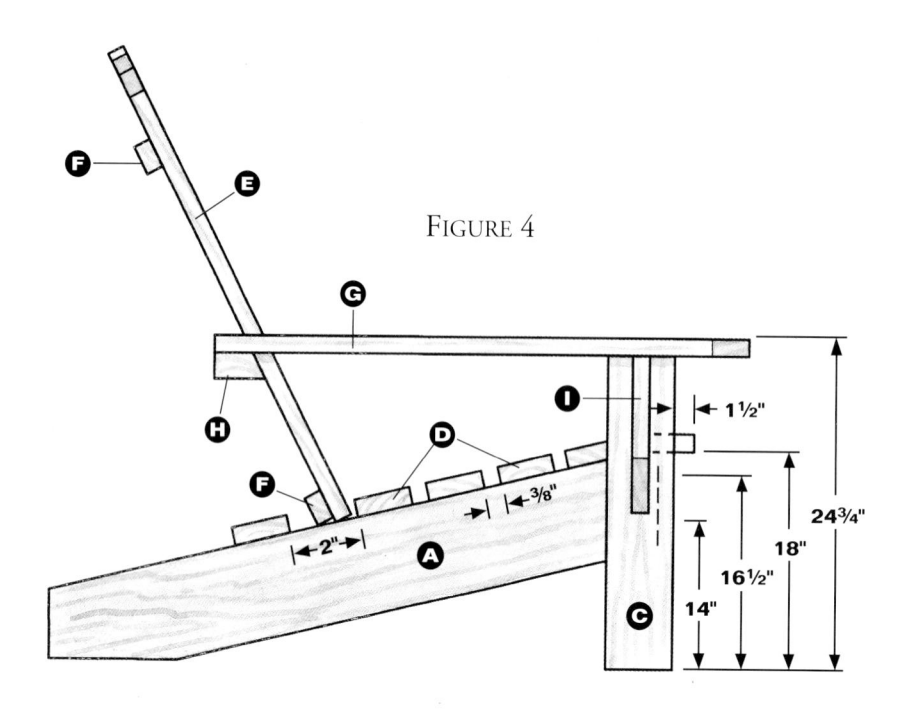

through the front and back legs, as shown in figure 2. Slip two 2-inch bolts through the holes at each joint, and tighten with washers and nuts.

5. Add the seat slats (D), starting with the front slat. Position the slat over the seat frame with its front edge overhanging the seat rail (B) by 1½ inches, as shown in figure 4. Secure the slat by driving two 1½-inch screws through the slat and into each of the three back legs (A), using a total of six screws per slat.

6. Add the next four seat slats (D) in the same manner as the first, spacing them roughly ⅜ inches apart. If necessary, place a pair of ⅜-inch-thick scrap wood blocks between the slats to help space them evenly.

7. Add the sixth seat slat (D), locating it 2 inches from the fifth slat, as shown in figure 4. This will leave a 2-inch space for installing the back assembly later.

8. On a flat work surface, place the eight back slats (E) over the two back rails (F), positioning the rails 19½ inches apart, with the bottom of the slats flush with the lower rail, as shown in figure 5. Space the back slats approximately ¼ inch apart, making sure the two outer slats are flush with the ends of the back rails. You can use some scrap wood spacers of the correct thickness to help with the slat spacing if you wish. Drive two 1¼-inch screws through each of the slats into each rail.

9. Find or make a thin, flexible stick of wood about 50 inches long, and use it to draw the curve at the top of the chair back. Hold or clamp the stick in the center of the back at the top, and flex it downward 6 inches at each side of the back, as shown in figure 5. Trace the curve onto the back, then saw to your line with the jigsaw. Smooth the saw marks with 150-grit sandpaper.

10. Cut the two arms (G) to the shape shown in figure 6, using the circular saw or a jigsaw. Use the first arm as a pattern to cut the second arm. Then smooth the sawn edges with 150-grit sandpaper.

11. Rip the 63° bevel on the arm rail (H), as shown in figure 7. If you have access to a table saw, tilt the blade to 27° on the bevel scale, and use the rip fence to cut the stock to the correct width. Or use a circular saw with the baseplate tilted to 27°, guiding the saw with a rip guide.

12. Position the arms over the rail, and use the square to check that the arms are 90° to the rail. Temporarily clamp the arms to the ends of the rail.

13. Although you can assemble the chair with the aid of bar clamps, it's easier on your back to enlist a helper. Begin by slipping the

back assembly into the 2-inch-wide gap in the seat slats. Then wrap the clamped arm assembly around the back of the bench, with the arms resting on the front legs. Have your friend sit in the bench, then adjust the arm assembly by repositioning the clamps until the arms are level with the floor and the back is sloped at a comfortable angle.

14 When you're satisfied with the sitting angle, screw through the arms (G), into the front legs (C), using three 1½-inch screws for each joint. Then screw through each back slat (E), into the upper back rail (F), using two 1½-inch screws per slat. Secure the back of the arms to the back rail (H) by drilling a ⅜-inch hole through each joint; then slip a 2½-inch bolt through the hole and tighten it with a washer and nut. Fasten the bottom of the back assembly by screwing at an angle through the lower back rail, into the edges of the back legs (A), using a 1½-inch screw for each joint.

15 Cut the two arm supports (I) as shown in figure 8. Cut the first support; then use it as a pattern to cut the second support. Before notching the supports for the bolt heads (see figures 2 and 8), position a support against a front leg (C), under the arm (G), and mark the bolt location on the support. Then saw the notch in each support with a jigsaw.

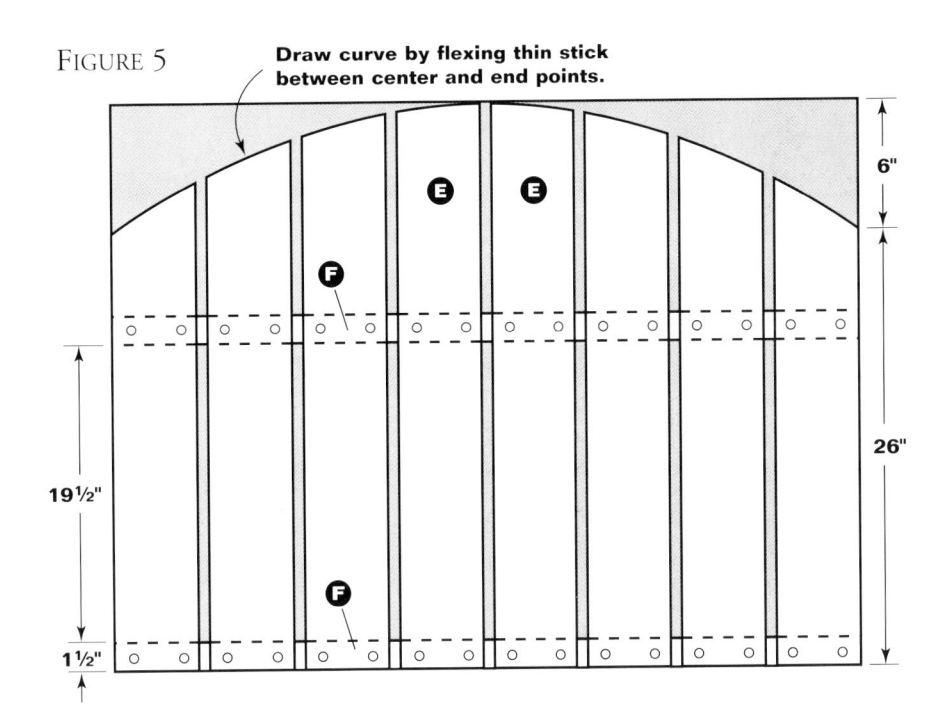

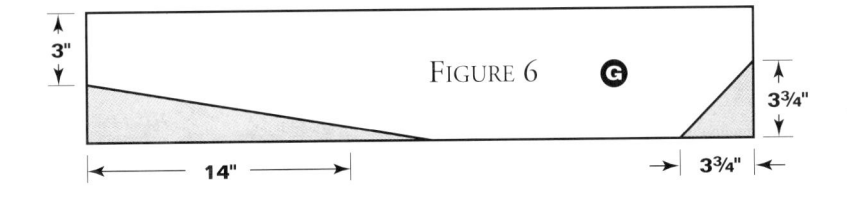

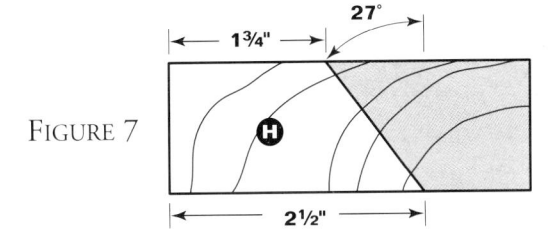

FIGURE 5

Draw curve by flexing thin stick between center and end points.

FIGURE 6

FIGURE 7

16 Finally, add the arm supports (I). Clamp each support under an arm (G), centering it on the front leg (C). Screw through the arm, into the support using a 1½-inch screw. Complete the chair by driving two 1½-inch screws through the inside of the front leg, into the support.

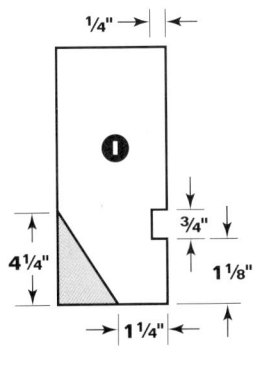

FIGURE 8

GARDEN FURNITURE

Building an Outdoor Table & Matching Chair

Relax and dine in your backyard or garden with this handsome table and matching chair. Simple in design and easy to build, they'll hold up beautifully outdoors thanks to their construction and the use of weather-resistant wood.

TIPS

- The projects shown are made from eucalyptus grandis, which holds up well outdoors and can be obtained from a sustainably-managed supply. See page 117 for alternative, decay-resistant woods.
- Simplify assembly by pre-boring all the joints for screws. (See page 97.)
- If you don't have a router and roundover bits, you can round the edges by hand with 150-grit sandpaper.

BUILDING AN OUTDOOR TABLE & MATCHING CHAIR | 105

MATERIALS AND TOOLS
For the table:

- 44 linear feet 1 x 6 eucalyptus grandis (see "Tips" on previous page)
- Scrap wood shims, 1/16 inch thick
- 12 #8 x 1¼" deck screws
- 44 #8 x 1½" deck screws
- 8 stainless-steel carriage bolts, ¼" x 2" with nuts and washers
- Power drill with #8 countersink and #8 pilot bit; ¼" drill bit
- #2 Phillips driver bit or Phillips-head screwdriver
- Circular saw
- Miter saw (optional)
- Router with ¼" and ⅜" roundover bits with ball bearings (optional)
- Bar-style clamps, 30 inches long
- 150-grit sandpaper

For one chair:

- 22 linear feet 1 x 6 eucalyptus grandis (see "Tips" on previous page)
- 14 #8 x 1¼" deck screws
- 58 #8 x 1½" deck screws
- 2 stainless-steel carriage bolts, ¼" x 2" with nuts and washers
- 2 stainless-steel carriage bolts, ⅜" x 2½" with nuts and washers
- Power drill with #8 countersink and #8 pilot bit; ¼" and ⅜" drill bits
- #2 Phillips driver bit or Phillips-head screwdriver
- Small square
- Circular saw
- Miter saw (optional)
- Router with ¼" roundover bit with ball bearing (optional)
- Scrap block of wood
- 150-grit sandpaper

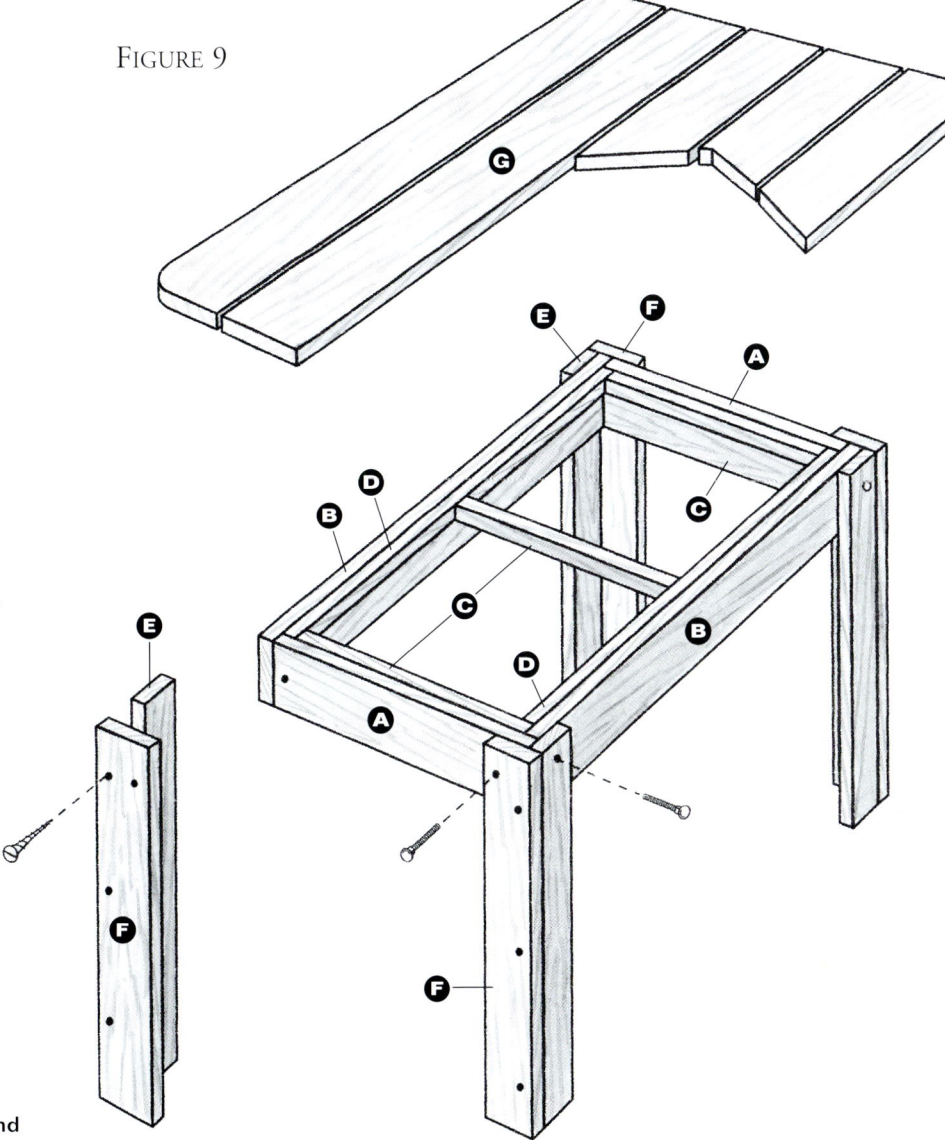

FIGURE 9

CUTTING LIST for the table:

CODE	DESCRIPTION	QTY.	MATERIAL	DIMENSIONS
A	Short rails	2	1 x 6	2¾" x 22¾"
B	Long rails	2	1 x 6	2¾" x 41½"
C	Short cleats	3	1 x 6	1" x 21¼"
D	Long cleats	2	1 x 6	1" x 40"
E	Narrow legs	4	1 x 6	2" x 29¼"
F	Wide legs	4	1 x 6	2¾" x 29¼"
G	Top boards	5	1 x 6	5½" x 45"

Instructions

For the table:

1. Cut parts A through F to the dimensions shown in the cutting list on the previous page.

2. Lay out the short and long rails (A and B) on the work surface, long rails overlapping the short rails, and joints flush. Drive two 1½-inch screws through each end of the long rails, into the endgrain of the short rails.

3. With the router and the ¼-inch roundover bit, soften the lower edge of the frame by routing the outside and inside faces.

4. Countersink for screws in the five cleat pieces (C and D), drilling holes through adjacent faces in each cleat as shown in figure 10. The only critical hole placement is in the short cleats (C), where the holes will align with the top boards (G) above.

5. Center one short cleat (C) between the two long cleats (D). Attach the pieces by driving a 1½-inch screw through each long cleat, into the ends of the short cleat. Check that this partial frame fits snug between the rail assembly, and correct if necessary.

6. Secure the assembled cleats to the rail assembly using 1¼-inch screws, aligning the cleats flush with the top of the rail assembly. Add the remaining two short cleats (C) in the same fashion.

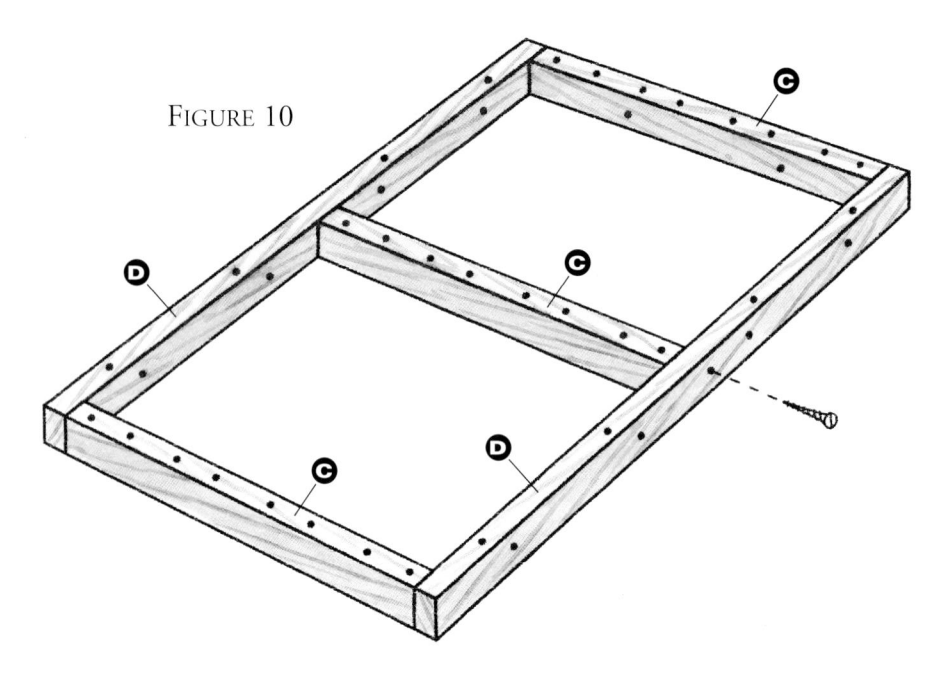

7. Assemble the narrow and wide leg pieces (E and F) into four legs, positioning each wide piece so it overlaps the narrow piece. Secure each leg by driving three 1½-inch screws evenly spaced through the wide piece, into the narrow piece. Roundover all but the top edges of each leg with a router and ¼-inch roundover bit.

8. With the frame assembly upside down, position a leg at each corner so the screws you installed in step 7 show at each end of the frame. Lay out the position of the bolt holes as shown in figure 11, and drill two ¼-inch holes through each leg and frame assembly, one hole on each adjacent face. Slip the carriage bolts through the holes and secure them with washers and nuts.

9. Cut the five top boards (G) to size. Lay them show-side down on the work surface, with their ends square to

FIGURE 10

FIGURE 11

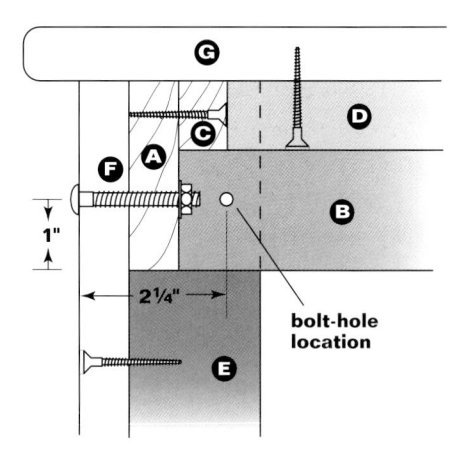

BUILDING AN OUTDOOR TABLE & MATCHING CHAIR 107

each other. Slip 1/16-inch-thick wood or cardboard shims between the boards to create a small gap between each board; then clamp the boards across their width. Center the base over the boards, with the boards extending past the base evenly on all sides. Secure the frame to the top boards using 1½-inch screws driven through the cleats, into the underside of the top.

10 Stand the table upright and round over the edges of the top by routing with a 3/8-inch roundover bit. Then position the tabletop on edge and rout a smaller roundover using the 1/4-inch roundover bit.

For the chair:

1 Cut all the chair parts (A through J) to the dimensions in the cutting list to the right. Leave the ends of the back supports (F) and the arm supports (H) square for now.

2 Lay out the side seat rails (A) and the front and back seat rails (B) on your work surface, with the side rails overlapping the front and back rails. Drive two 1½-inch screws through each end of the side rails, into the endgrain of the front and back rails. Be sure to assemble the joints flush.

CUTTING LIST for the chair:

CODE	DESCRIPTION	QTY.	MATERIAL	DIMENSIONS
A	Side seat rails	2	1 x 6	3" x 17"
B	Front & back seat rails	2	1 x 6	3" x 18½"
C	Seat slats	6	1 x 6	2⅝" x 20"
D	Narrow legs	4	1 x 6	2" x 17¼"
E	Wide legs	4	1 x 6	2¾" x 17¼"
F	Back supports	2	1 x 6	2" x 21" to long point of miter
G	Back slats	3	1 x 6	2⅝" x 21½"
H	Arm support	2	1 x 6	1¼" x 16½" to long point of miter
I	Arm post	2	1 x 6	2" x 11"
J	Arm	2	1 x 6	2⅝" x 18"

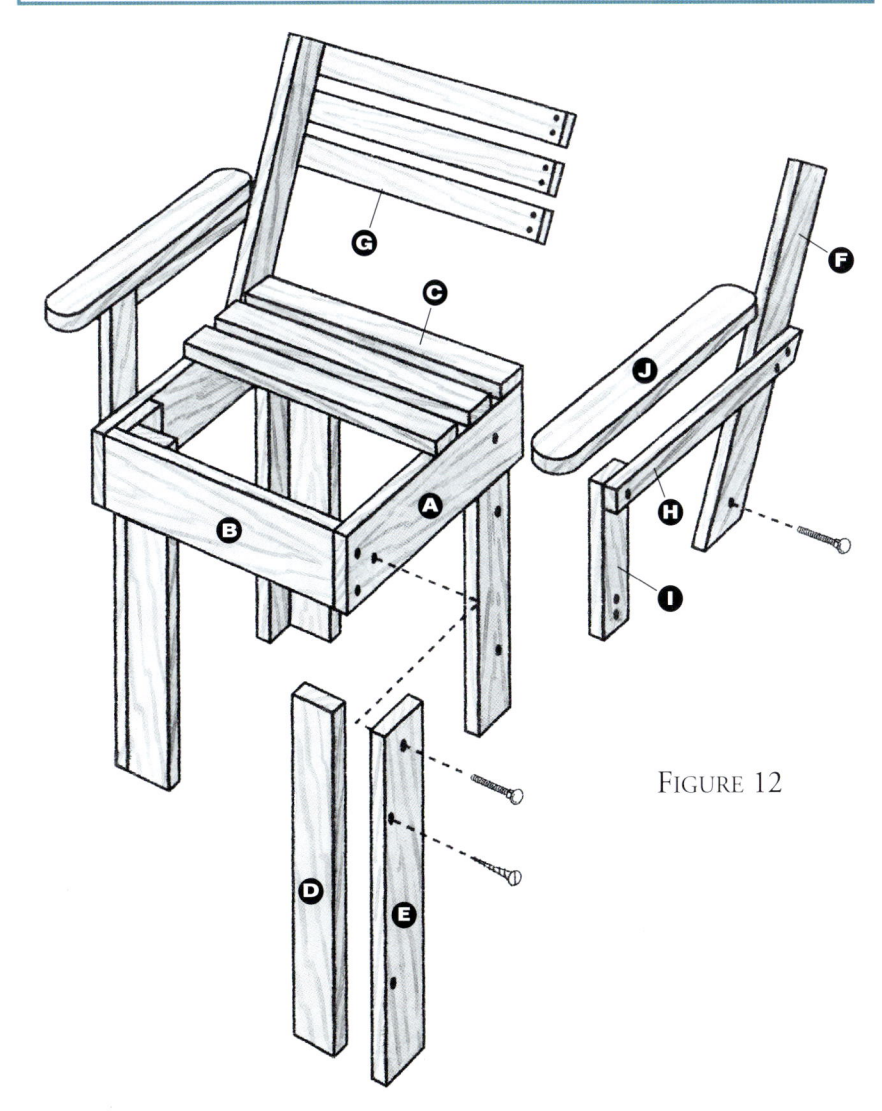

FIGURE 12

3 Attach all the seat slats (C) to the assembled seat frame. Start with the front slat, positioning it on the frame so it overhangs the front of the frame by ¼ inch. Secure the slat to the top of the frame using two 1½-inch screws through each end of the slat. Secure a second slat flush to the back of the frame, using two screws per end. Attach the remaining slats, spacing them equally by eye, with about ¼ inch between them.

4 For each leg, position a wide leg piece (E) over a narrow piece (D) and screw through the wide piece, into the narrow piece, forming an L shape. Use two 1½-inch screws for each leg assembly, spacing them evenly.

5 Turn the seat frame upside down, with the slats facing the workbench. Position a leg into each inside corner of the frame. The screws you installed in the legs in step 4 should face the sides of the seat frame. Drill ¼-inch holes through the frame and front legs, locating the holes as shown in figure 13. Then secure each front leg to the seat frame with a single ¼ x 2-inch carriage bolt slipped through the hole. Tighten the bolt with a washer and nut. Then set the back legs aside.

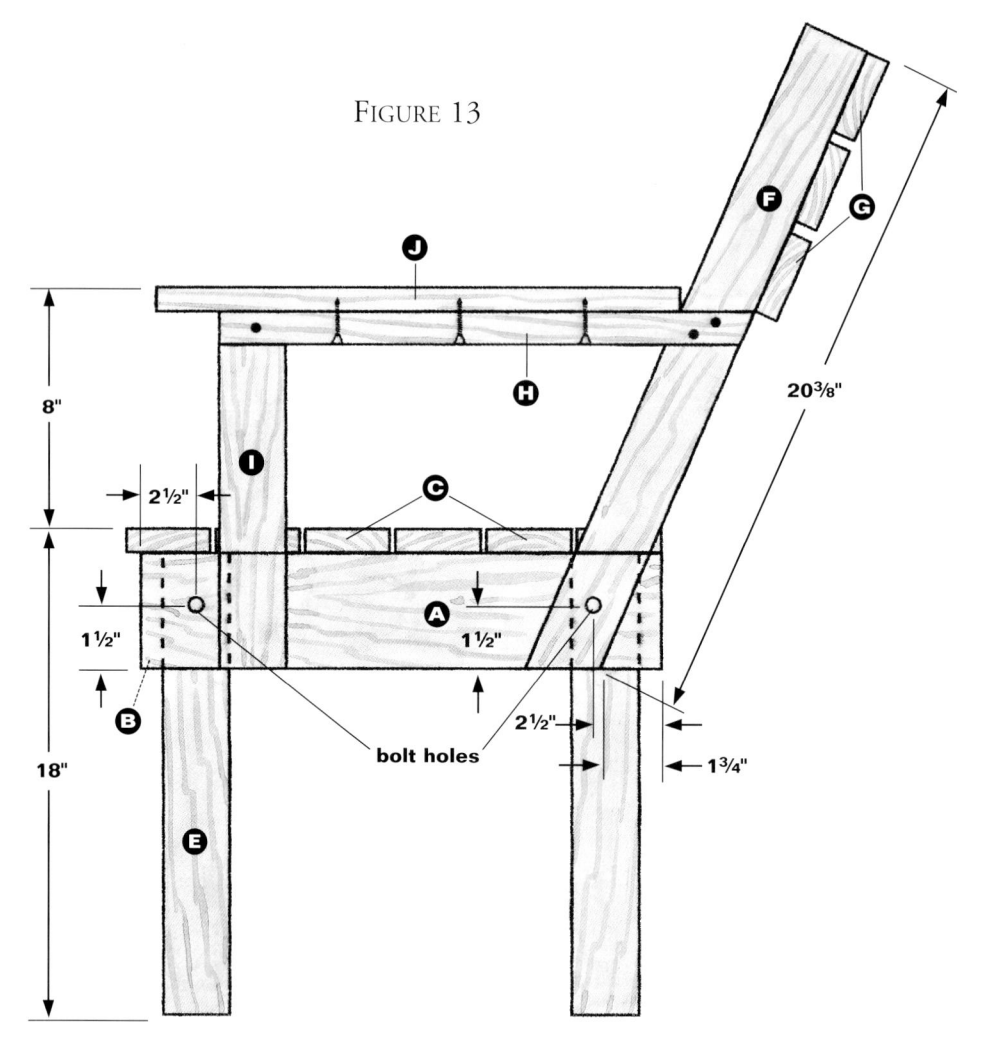

FIGURE 13

6 On each back support (F), mark one long edge at 20⅜ inch, as shown in figure 13; then draw an angled line from this point to the opposite corner. Cut the miter with the circular saw or on the miter saw.

7 Attach the back slats (G) to the back supports (F), starting with the top slat. Align the first slat flush with the ends and outside faces of the arm supports. Secure it to the supports using two 1½-inch screws at each end of the slat. Attach the other two slats the same way, leaving a ½-inch gap between the slats.

8 To attach the back legs and the back assembly to the seat frame, start by positioning the seat frame on its side. Place the legs on the inside back corners of the frame; then slip the back assembly over the outside of the frame so that the mitered end of the back support (F) is flush to the bottom of the frame and 1¾ inch in from the back of the frame, as shown in figure 13. Secure the back support with two 1¼-inch screws; then drill a ⅜-inch hole through each back support, frame and leg, locating the hole as shown in figure 13. Secure each back support and leg with a ⅜ x 2½-inch carriage bolt through the hole. Secure the bolt with a washer and nut.

9 On one long edge of each arm support (H), measure 16¼ inch from one end and draw an angled line from your mark to the opposite corner. Cut the miter with a circular saw or the miter saw. Countersink and drill three pilot holes through the underside of each support, as shown in figure 13.

10 Attach the arm posts (I) to each arm support (H) at right angles to the square end of the support, as shown in figure 13. Check the arrangement for square. Secure the joint with a 1¼-inch screw, making sure to assemble "right" and "left" support assemblies for the two sides of the chair.

11 Position each support assembly on the side of the seat frame, with the bottom of the arm post (H) flush to the bottom of the frame and 2¾ inches in from the front, as shown in figure 13. Check that the arm support (H) is level with the seat, and the miter at the back of the support is flush with the angled back support (F). Secure each assembly with two 1¼-inch screws through the post, into the frame, and two 1¼-inch screws through the arm support, into the back support.

12 Round the four corners of each arm (J) as shown in figure 12, using a sanding block made from sandpaper wrapped around a block of hard wood. Position the arm over the arm support (H), with its back butted against the back support (F) and overhanging the inside face of the post by about ¼ inch. Secure the arms by driving three 1½-inch screws through each arm support, into the underside of each arm.

APPENDIX A
When to Bring in the Professionals

Very few things in life are as rewarding as creating something yourself, and all of the projects in this book are well within reach of the average DIYer. Nevertheless, there will be times when you may feel overwhelmed by a large task—in particular, building a wall or creating a path can take more than a few casual weekend hours. If you're wondering whether or not you should bring in professional help, here are a few tips:

CONSIDER HIRING A PROFESSIONAL IF:

- Your free time is your most valuable commodity. Remember that most DIY projects take longer than you may originally anticipate.
- The project requires specialized skills, such as the use of heavy equipment or electric wiring. Many specialized tasks can be dangerous if you haven't had proper training.
- Your body's not up to the assignment. Laying a heavy stone path, digging postholes, and many other DIY activities can be tough on *anyone's* back and knees and may leave muscles aching.
- The project needs to be completed within a set amount of time. A professional's job is to get your project done on time. Your job may demand extra hours just when you need to spend them on your backyard project.
- Building codes in your area specify that the kind of project you're considering must be built by a professional. Walls over 3 or 4 feet tall are one example.

APPENDIX B
More about Stone

Whether you're building a stone path or a stone wall, there will be times when the pieces won't fit the way you'd like them to. You have three options: Buy or gather at least 35 percent more stone than you think you'll need so you'll always have extras to choose from; hire a masonry professional to help with large volumes of cutting and trimming, and to make curved or specialty cuts; or cut and trim the stone yourself. Overbuying will add to the expense of your project, but you may be able to use the excess for other projects. Hiring a professional will also add to the cost, but will save you time and effort—and it's your only option if you have to make curved cuts. Trimming stone, however, is fairly easy; and, if you're comfortable with a circular saw, you can make simple straight cuts yourself, too.

TOOLS AND MATERIALS FOR TRIMMING AND CUTTING STONE

- Square (to use as a straight edge)
- Brick chisel (for scoring stone and for breaking off larger portions of stone)
- Cold chisel (for trimming finer portions of stone)
- Garden hose with nozzle
- Double-insulated circular saw (Make absolutely sure your saw is double insulated—and thus safe for use around water—before using it for cutting stone.)
- 3-pound mason's hammer
- Length of 2 x 4 lumber
- Safety glasses
- Ear protection
- Heavy-duty gloves

INSTRUCTIONS FOR TRIMMING STONE

To make a stone fit more tightly in a wall or to clean up a stone's face (the portion that shows on the surface of a wall or path), you may want to trim it. Here's how (refer to figure 1):

1 Place the stone to be trimmed on a steady work bench, positioning it so it's sitting the way you want it to sit in the wall. Pull it out slightly so the face to be trimmed overhangs the edge of the bench slightly. Your goal is to trim any bulges or protrusions from this face so it's flush with the bench edge.

FIGURE 1

2 Next, mark where you'll need to chisel to create a smooth face. Using your square as a straight edge score a line with your brick chisel around the stone's sides and top; this line should be even with the bench edge. Turn the stone over and mark the bottom surface the same way.

3 Wearing safety glasses and heavy-duty gloves, make preparatory fractures in the stone. Place your brick chisel on top of the scored line. Tap the chisel lightly with your mason's hammer, moving the chisel along the entire line. Repeat on all four sides. Go around the stone with your chisel and hammer once more to deepen the fracture.

4 Now, trim the stone. Place your brick chisel in the fracture and strike it with enough force to break off shards of rock. Move around the fracture line, turning the stone as necessary.

5 Clean up ragged edges on the stone with your cold chisel. Just position the chisel against the portion to be trimmed and tap it lightly with the mason's hammer.

The stone sold at your local stone yard will almost certainly have been quarried nearby. Check with your supplier to find out what kind of stone is common to your region.

INSTRUCTIONS FOR CUTTING STONES

Use this technique to cut a flat stone, such as a paver for a path, across its grain. (Refer to figure 2.)

1. Using the straight edge as a guide, score a line across the surface of the stone with the brick chisel to indicate where you'll make the cut.

2. Place the stone on your work surface, propping it so it sits at a slight angle. Secure the nozzle of the hose on the stone so you can run water over the scored line in a slow, steady stream as you make the cut. (The water will keep the cut clear and stone dust to a minimum so you can see what you're doing.) If you're using an extension cord with your double-insulated circular saw, waterproof the joint where the saw cord plugs into the extension cord by wrapping it in duct tape.

3. Put on your safety glasses and ear protection. Hold the circular saw with its guide mark right over the scored line and its blade just above—but not touching—the stone. Turn the saw on and carefully lower it until the blade hits the scored line. Gently move the blade back and forth, letting the weight of the saw do the cutting. Cut the scored line to a depth of between ¼ to ½ inch along its entire length.

4. When you've completed the cut, place the length of 2 x 4 lumber on your work surface. Position the stone on top of it, with the edge of the scored line aligned with one edge of the 2 x 4; the width of the 2 x 4 should be under the part of the stone you want to keep. Using the hammer, press or lightly tap the stone at the center of the portion you want to remove; it should snap right off.

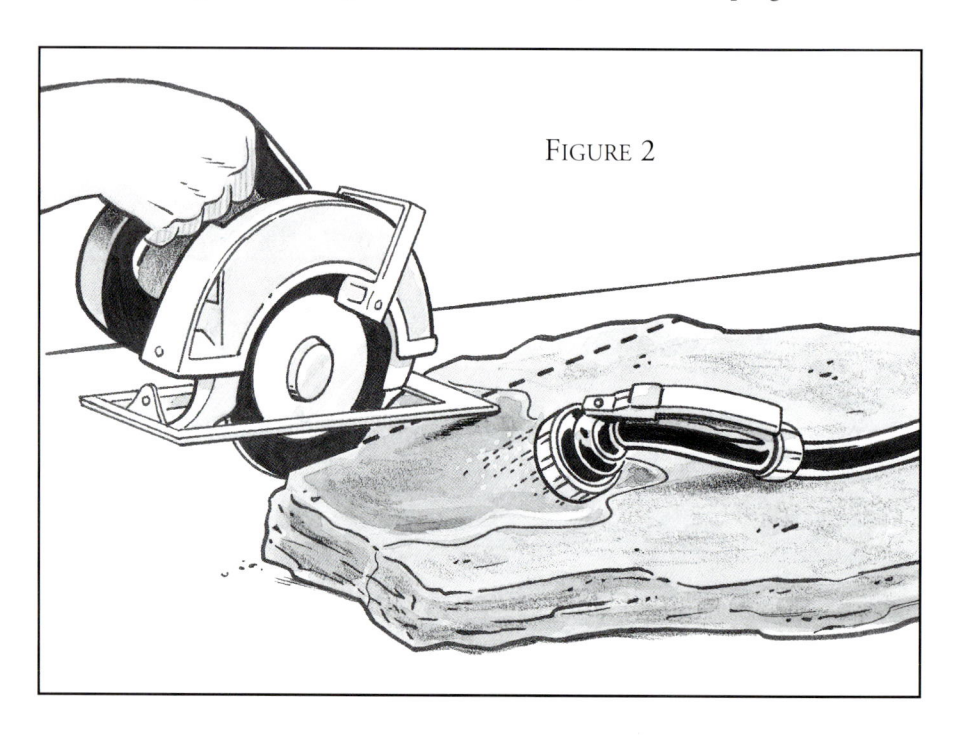

FIGURE 2

MORE ABOUT BRICK 113

Appendix B.1
Characteristics of Common Stone

STONE	WEIGHT RELATIVE TO SIZE	COLOR	WORKABILITY	STRENGTH
Basalt	Heavy	Grey, black, and brown	MODERATE	Excellent
Gneiss	Medium	Pinkish-grey, black, white, and banded	GOOD	Good
Granite	Heavy	Pale grey, pink, and red	DIFFICULT	Excellent
Limestone	Heavy	Pale green, grey, buff, white, and black	MODERATE TO EXCELLENT	Good to excellent
Sandstone (dense)	Medium	Grey and brown	GOOD	Good to excellent
Slate	Medium	Black, green, red, blue, dark grey	GOOD	Good for paving

Appendix C
More about Brick

CUTTING BRICK

When you're laying a path or building a wall from brick, you may need to cut bricks to fit your pattern. Most bricks can be split easily with hand tools, using the technique described here. However, if you need to cut a large number of bricks or make very precise or angled cuts, consider renting a water-cooled masonry saw to do the job.

TOOLS AND MATERIALS FOR CUTTING BRICK
- Chalk
- Straight edge
- Brick chisel (sometimes called a "brick sett")
- 3-pound mason's hammer
- Solid, steady work surface
- Safety glasses
- Heavy-duty gloves

1 With chalk and a straight edge, mark a line around all four surfaces of the brick indicating the cut line.

2 Place the brick on a steady, solid work surface. (The sand bed for a dry-laid brick path makes an excellent surface for cutting brick.)

3 Center the brick chisel over the cut line and tap it gently but firmly until the brick splits. If the brick doesn't split after the third tap, turn it over, place the brick chisel on the cut line and strike it with a little more force until it breaks.

No matter how well you've planned a pattern for your brick wall or path, there will be times when you must cut a brick to fit.

Appendix C.1
Types of Brick

Brick comes in a variety of types, sizes, colors, and textures, many designed for specific purposes. The chart below covers the types of brick best for the projects in this book. Remember that brick is manufactured locally, so you'll probably find some variation in the standard dimensions given here. Take the brick's actual size into account when you purchase for a specific project, and, if you're mortaring the bricks, factor in the size of mortar joints, too.

TYPE	ACTUAL DIMENSIONS* (IN INCHES)	COMMENTS/RECOMMENDED USES
Common (or building) brick		Usually red or pink. Solid- and hollow-core styles available.
SW (severe weather)	2¼ x 3¾ x 8	For outdoor use in projects where bricks are in contact with the ground.
MW (medium weather)	2¼ x 3¾ x 8	For outdoor use in projects subject to freezing, but where brick is not in contact with ground.
NW (no weather)	2¼ x 3¾ x 8	For indoor use only.
Face brick		Higher quality than common brick. Recommended for use in outside walls. Solid- and hollow-core styles available.
Standard	2¼ x 3¾ x 8	
Oversize	3½ x 3 x 9½	
Norman	2½ x 3½ x 11½	
Modular	3½ x 3 x 11½	
Jumbo	3½ x 3½ x 11½	
Paver brick		High-quality brick designed for use in paths, walkways, patios, and driveways.
Standard	2¼ x 3¾ x 8	
Split	1¼ x 3¾ x 8	
Mortarless	2 x 4 x 8	
Economy	1½ x 3½ x 11½	

*Brick is sometimes labeled by its nominal dimensions, which account for the thickness of a mortar joint. The actual dimensions of a brick will be either ⅜ inch or ½ inch less than indicated by the nominal dimensions. If you call your brick supplier for a quote, be sure to ask whether the dimensions quoted are nominal or actual.

Appendix D
More about Woodworking for Outdoor Use

The biggest concern you'll face when building a wooden project for outdoor use is weather resistance. Although all wood will eventually succumb to rot and decay, you do have several options for increasing the weather resistance of your handiwork. These include using naturally weather-resistant lumber, chemically treated lumber, and the application of protective finishes.

FINISHES

Finishing is the final step before putting a project out in the garden for years of enjoyment. In fact, proper finishing can add to those years significantly. All finishes are available in latex (or water-based) and alkyd (the modern equivalent of oil-based) formulations. Latex finishes are easier to apply and dry much faster, but alkyds last longer and offer a greater degree of protection.

Water Sealers

Most water sealers available today are "penetrating finishes," meaning they penetrate the surface of the wood and offer a high degree of protection. Of the types of finishes listed here, sealers have the least affect on wood's appearance. They're often used to weather-proof decks and railings, and make a good choice for projects made from attractive woods. Water sealers range in appearance from muted and barely perceptible to smooth and semi-gloss sheens. Be sure to buy a finish sealer rather than a clear sanding sealer. Water sealers should be reapplied on a yearly basis.

Stains

Stains come in a huge variety of colors and styles, ranging from almost translucent to nearly opaque. Many are also available in penetrating formulations and contain a sealer; these are the best choices for outdoor projects. (Stains that don't contain a sealer won't offer protection from the elements.) Stains don't require a primer of any kind, and one coat usually offers sufficient protection against water damage. Stains should be reapplied every two to three years.

Paints

A few coats of paint can turn a project made from unattractive wood into a gorgeous show piece. Choose from high-gloss enamels, flat-sheen paints with a matte finish, and several styles in between. Just make sure to buy an exterior-grade formulation. Look for a warranty, too; this will tell you approximately how many years the paint will last.

All paints require a primer. This essential base coat will seal the wood's surface and aid in the paint's adhesion. Be sure to match the primer and paint types: You must use a latex primer with latex paint and an alkyd primer with alkyd paint.

Applying Finishes

Choose a well-ventilated area for applying finishes, and protect your work surface with a layer of newspaper. Make sure the project is sanded to a smooth finish and is completely clean and dry. Each type and brand of finish varies slightly, so always read the manufacturer's instructions; they'll tell you how long the finish will take to dry and whether a second or third coat is necessary. They may also recommend a preferred type of applicator. If not, just use a good-quality synthetic brush made from nylon or polyester; inexpensive, disposable foam brushes offer another good option.

APPENDIX D.1
Properties of Common Woods for Outdoor Use

	WOOD	WEATHER RESISTANCE	EXPENSE	RECOMMENDED FINISH	ADDITIONAL COMMENTS
Tropical Hardwoods	Teak	Highly resistant	Very expensive	No finish necessary	Typically available only through specialty lumber suppliers.
	Mahogany	Highly resistant	Very expensive	No finish necessary	Typically available only through specialty lumber suppliers.
Softwoods	Redwood	Good resistance	Very expensive	Water sealer	Scarce and environmentally threatened.
	Western red cedar	Good resistance	Moderate	Water sealer or transparent stain	Very common, easy to find at local lumberyards (not as readily available through national chains).
	Pressure-treated southern yellow pine	Highly resistant	Inexpensive	Semi-transparent stain (paint won't adhere to pressure-treated wood)	Contains harmful chemicals (such as arsenic), and should not be used to build picnic tables or projects for children.
	Atlantic cypress	Good resistance	Moderate	Water sealer or transparent stain	Readily available in the southeastern United States at local lumberyards, but difficult to find in other parts of the country.
	Western white cedar	Good resistance	Moderate	Water sealer or transparent stain	Easy to find at local lumberyards (not as readily available through national chains).
	Douglas fir	Fair	Inexpensive	Semi-transparent stain or paint	Readily available, but must be finished properly to ensure good weather resistance.
	Southern yellow pine, spruce, and white pine	Poor	Inexpensive	Paint or semi-transparent sealer	Readily available, but won't hold up well to weather unless carefully finished.
Hardwoods	White oak	Fair	Moderate	Must be painted for outdoor use	Splinters easily, making it a poor choice for outdoor use.
	Red oak	Poor	Moderate	Must be painted for outdoor use	Not recommended for outdoor use.
	Walnut	Poor	Expensive	Must be painted for outdoor use	Rots easily, not recommended for outdoor use.

Appendix E
Softwood Lumber Sizes

You'll buy softwoods as dimension lumber—boards that have been dried, planed to a standard thickness, and cut to a standard width. These processes can reduce a board's original dimensions by as much as ¾ inch. The confusing thing about dimension lumber is that it's named for its nominal (pre dried, pre planed) thickness and width. If you ask for a 2 x 4 ("two by four"), you won't get a board that's 2 inches thick and 4 inches wide. Instead, you'll get a board that's about 1½ inches thick and 3½ inches wide. Keep in mind that boards of the same nominal size can vary as much as ⅛ inch in width or thickness; measuring lumber before you buy it will save troublesome errors during assembly. The chart to the right gives the actual dimensions of common nominal dimension lumber.

Nominal	Actual
1 x 2	¾" x 1½"
1 x 4	¾" x 3½"
1 x 6	¾" x 5½"
1 x 8	¾" x 7¼"
1 x 10	¾" x 9¼"
1 x 12	¾" x 11¼"
2 x 2	1½" x 1½"
2 x 4	1½" x 3½"
2 x 6	1½" x 5½"
2 x 8	1½" x 7¼"
2 x 10	1½" x 9¼"
2 x 12	1½" x 11¼"
4 x 4	3½" x 3½"
4 x 6	3½" x 5½"
6 x 6	5½" x 5½"
8 x 8	7½" x 7½"

Appendix F
Metric Conversions

Length

Inches	CM
⅛	0.3
¼	0.6
⅜	1.0
½	1.3
⅝	1.6
¾	1.9
⅞	2.2
1	2.5
1¼	3.2
1½	3.8
1¾	4.4
2	5.1
2½	6.4
3	7.6
3½	8.9
4	10.2
4½	11.4
5	12.7
6	15.2
7	17.8
8	20.3
9	22.9
10	25.4
11	27.9
12	30.5
13	33.0
14	35.6
15	38.1
16	40.6
17	43.2
18	45.7
19	48.3
20	50.8
21	53.3
22	55.9
23	58.4
24	61.0
25	63.5
26	66.0
27	68.6
28	71.1
29	73.7
30	76.2
31	78.7
32	81.3
33	83.8
34	86.4
35	88.9
36	91.4
37	94.0
38	96.5
39	99.1
40	101.6
41	104.1
42	106.7
43	109.2
44	111.8
45	114.3
46	116.8
47	119.4
48	121.9
49	124.5
50	127.0

Volume

1 fluid ounce = 29.6 ml
1 pint = 473 ml
1 quart = 946 ml
1 gallon (128 fl. oz.) = 3.785 liters

liters x .2642 = gallons
liters x 2.11 = pints
liters x 33.8 = fluid ounces
gallons x 3.785 = liters
gallons x .1337 = cubic feet
cubic feet x 7.481 = gallons
cubic feet x 28.32 = liters

Weight

0.035 ounces = 1 gram
1 ounce = 28.35 grams
1 pound = 453.6 grams

grams x .0353 = ounces
grams x .0022 = pounds
ounces x 28.35 = grams
pounds x 453.6 = grams
tons (short) x 907.2 = kilograms
tons (metric) x 2205 = pounds
kilograms x .0011 = tons (short)
pounds x .00045 = tons (metric)

USDA HARDINESS-ZONE MAP 119

APPENDIX G
Hardiness-Zone Map

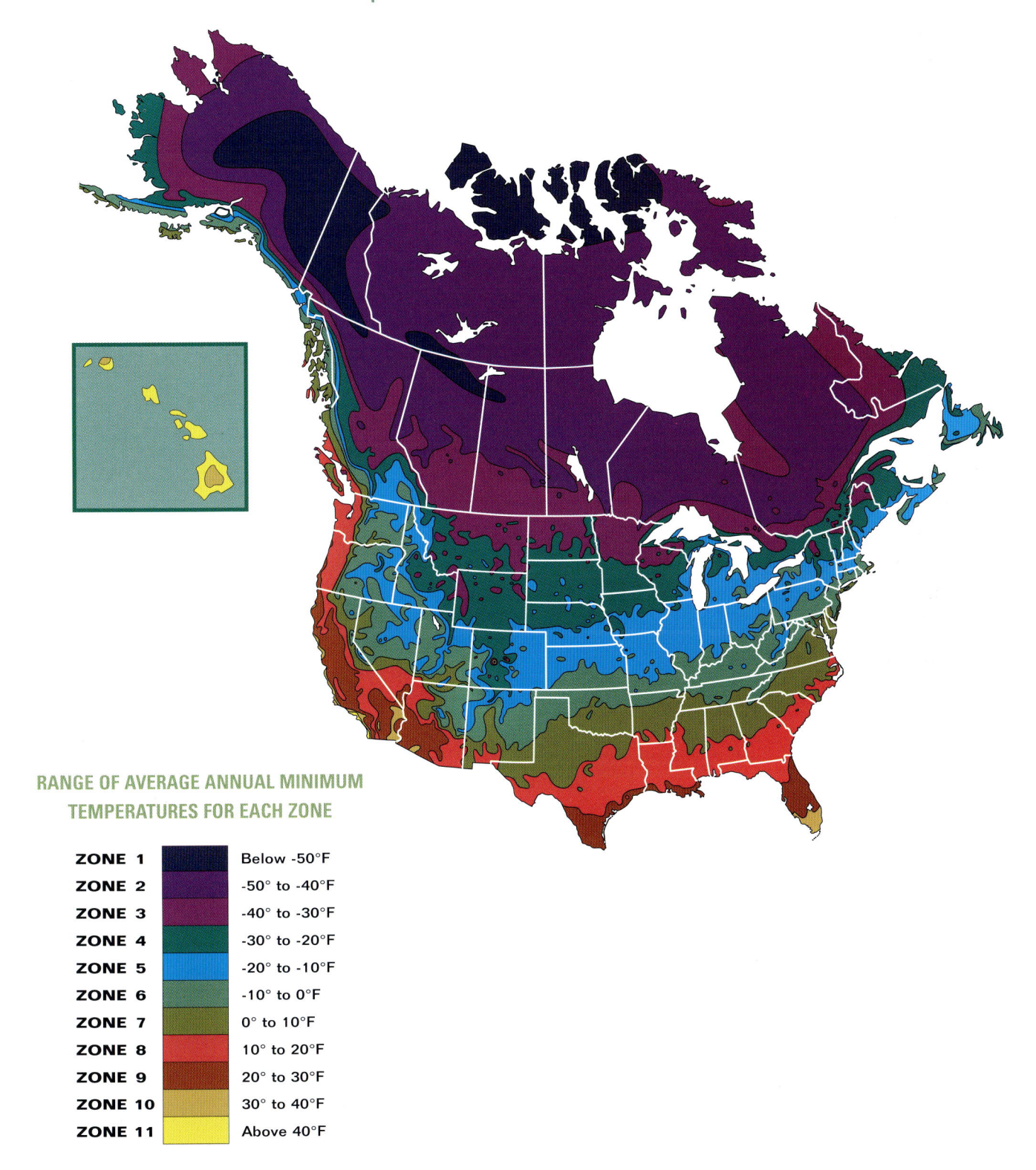

RANGE OF AVERAGE ANNUAL MINIMUM TEMPERATURES FOR EACH ZONE

ZONE 1	Below -50°F
ZONE 2	-50° to -40°F
ZONE 3	-40° to -30°F
ZONE 4	-30° to -20°F
ZONE 5	-20° to -10°F
ZONE 6	-10° to 0°F
ZONE 7	0° to 10°F
ZONE 8	10° to 20°F
ZONE 9	20° to 30°F
ZONE 10	30° to 40°F
ZONE 11	Above 40°F

Acknowledgements

CONSULTATION
For their expert advice:
Matt Fuscoe (Scott R. Melrose & Associates, P.A., Asheville, N.C.)
Bo Harper (Bo Scapes Personal Gardening Service, Pickens, S.C.)

PHOTOGRAPHY
Many thanks to Richard Hasselburg, for his good humor, flexible schedule, and great eye. The following photos are by Mr. Hasselburg:
Pages 8; 9 (bottom); 10; 11; 13; 14; 16; 18; 20 (bottom); 23 (right); 26; 27 (top and bottom); 28 (right); 29; 31; 33; 38; 39; 41 (top); 48; 49 (top and bottom); 61; 66; 67; 68 (top); 69; 71 (top); 74 (right, top and bottom); 75 (left and right, bottom); 78; 80 (bottom); 83; 84; 85 (left); 90; 91 (all); 93; 94; 95; 96; 98; 100; 104; 109; 110; 112 (all); 115 (all); and 116.

Warm thanks also to Evan Bracken, with whom photo shoots are always a pleasure—even on 100° days in South Carolina. The following photos are by Mr. Bracken:
Pages 9 (top); 17; 20 (top); 28 (left); 35; 43 (bottom); 44; 52 (bottom); 60; 70; 74 (bottom, left); 75 (top); 92; 113 and (all).

And to Thom Gaines, who not only designed and laid out this book, but also took the following photos:
Pages 9 (center); 12; 19; 23 (left); 28 (right); 32; 40; 41 (bottom); 43 (center); 46; 52 (top); 54; and 88.

ADDITIONAL PHOTO CREDITS
Thanks also to the following photographers for contributing images for inclusion:
Julie Sprott/gardenIMAGE, page 42; Jane O'Neil Spector, pages 43 (top) and 68 (bottom, left); Hollingsworth (for the U.S. Fish and Wildlife Service), pages 71 (center), 76, 82, and 85 (center); S. Maslowski (for the U.S. Fish and Wildlife Service), pages 71 (bottom) and 80 (top); Michelle Keenan and Rosebud the One-Eared Wonder Cat, page 72; R.H. Barrett (for the U.S. Fish and Wildlife Service), page 73; John Oberheur (for the U.S. Fish and Wildlife Service), page 77; Nan Rollison (for the U.S. Fish and Wildlife Service), page 81; and Glen Smart (for the U.S. Fish and Wildlife Service), page 85 (right).

LOCATIONS
Many thanks to the following individuals and businesses for allowing us to photograph their beautiful gardens and grounds:
Judi and Bill Ayers (The Wright Inn & Carriage House, Asheville, N.C.); Beaufort House Victorian Bed & Breakfast, Asheville, N.C.; Jack and Joyce Clarkson (Greenville, S.C.); Stewart and Gay Coleman (Asheville, N.C.); John Cram (Kenilworth Gardens, Asheville, N.C.); Raymond and Eve Cruitt (Asheville, N.C.); Elizabeth Eve (Asheville, N.C.); Victor and Sharon Fahrer (Asheville, N.C.); Hedy Fischer and Randy Shull (Asheville, N.C.); Catty and Thom Gaines (Black Mountain, N.C.); Dr. Peter and Jasmin Gentling (Asheville, N.C.); Bo and Linda Harper (Bo Scapes Personal Gardening Service, Pickens, S.C.); Anne Jones (Asheville, N.C.); Bill and Pat Kwehl (Asheville, N.C.); Graham A. Kimak (Easely, S.C.); Barbara and William Lewin (Asheville, N.C.); Susan and Michael McBride (Asheville, N.C.); Stewart and Jean McLennan (Black Mountain, N.C.); Christopher D. Mello (Horticulturist, Asheville, N.C.); Phyllis R. Mykleby (Black Mountain, N.C.); North Carolina Arboretum (Asheville, N.C., www.ncarboretum.org); Ed and Trena Parker (Asheville, N.C.); J. Dabney Peeples Design Associates (landscape architects, Easely, S.C.); Martha Peiser (Asheville, N.C.); Richmond Hill Inn (Asheville, N.C.); Paul and Hazel Sanger ("Carlsbad," Highlands, N.C.); Colleen Sikes (Asheville, N.C.); Cathy and Larry Sklar (The Albermarle Inn, Asheville, N.C.); Dr. James and

Joanna Sloan (Asheville, N.C.); Glen and Jan Spears (Greenville, S.C.); J. R. Stone Sales, Inc. (Asheville, N.C.); Ali Lingerfelt-Tait and Jeffrey Tait (Asheville, N.C.); Taylor and Webb's (Asheville, N.C.); Dr. Peter and Cathy Wallenborn (Asheville, N.C.); and Lisa and Rice Yordy (The Lion & the Rose Bed & Breakfast), Asheville, N.C.).

PROJECT DESIGN

Thanks to the folks who designed and built projects:

Joe Archibald (Arc Design Woodworking/Design·Build, Asheville, N.C.), who built the portable deck squares (pages 98 through 99) and the Adirondack love seat (pages 100 through 103).

Robin Clark (Robin's Wood Ltd. Manufacturer), who created the bat house (pages 78 through 79), the butterfly box (pages 88 through 89); and the outdoor table and matching chair (pages 104 through 109).

Terry Taylor, for sharing his mosaic bird bath (pages 83 through 84).

ILLUSTRATIONS

Special thanks to Orrin Lundgreen for creating the illustrations on the following pages, always under tight deadlines and with a good sense of humor: 21; 22; 24; 25 (top and bottom); 26; 27; 31; 47; 53 (top and bottom); 55; 56; 57; 59; 62; 63; 65; 79; 89; 99; 101; 102; 103; 105; 106; 107; 108; and 111.

Warm thanks also to Lorraine Plaxico for her watercolor illustrations, which appear on pages 30; 34; 36; 37; 40; 50; 58; 64; and 86.

RESEARCH AND WRITING

A lot of research goes into a book of this nature. Thanks to the following people for lending their skills: Carey Burda (Mars Hill, N.C.), for her research on coyotes; Holly Cowart (Brevard, N.C.), for her research on outdoor furniture; Marcianne Miller (Asheville, N.C.), for researching and writing the rough drafts of chapters 3 and 4; Andy Rae (Asheville, N.C.), for editing the instructions for all the woodworking projects; and Kendrick Weeks (Raleigh, N.C.), for his research on backyard birds.

AND...

For their good humor and support, thanks to the entire staff at Lark Books (Asheville, N.C.), and to our managing editor at Time-Life, Linda Bellamy.

Bibliography

Adams, George. *Birdscaping your Garden: a Practical Guide to Backyard Birds and the Plants that Attract Them.* Emmaus, Pa: Rodale Press, 1994.

Appleton, Bonnie Lee and Alfred F. Scheider. *Rodale's Successful Organic Gardening: Trees, Shrubs, and Vines.* Emmaus, Pa: Rodale Press, Inc., 1993.

Barrett, Jim. *Fences, Gates, and Trellises: Plan, Design, Build.* Upper Saddle River, N.J.: Creative Homeowner, 1998.

Barrett, Jim. *Quick Guide: Fences & Gates.* Upper Saddle River, N.J.: Creative Home Owner Press, 1998.

Bartholomew, Mel. *Square Foot Gardening.* Emmaus, Pa.: Rodale Press, 1981.

Bender, Steve, ed. *The Southern Living®Garden Book.* Birmingham, Ala.: Oxmoor House, 1998.

Bird, Richard. *Fences and Hedges and Other Garden Dividers.* New York: Stewart, Tabori & Chang, 1998.

Blomgren, Paige Gilchrist. *Making Paths & Walkways: Creative Ideas and Simple Techniques.* Asheville, N.C.: Lark Books, 1999.

Brickell, Christopher and Judith D. Zuk, eds. *The American Horticultural Society A—Z Encyclopedia of Garden Plants.* New York: DK Publishing, 1996.

Burda, Cindy. *Weekend Woodworking for the Garden.* New York: Sterling Publishing, Co., 2000.

———. *Cooking and Dining Outdoors.* Alexandria, Va: Time-Life Books, 2000.

Buscher, Fred K. and Susan McClure. *All About Pruning.* San Ramon, Calif.: Ortho Books, 1989.

Cox, Jeff. *Decorating Your Garden.* New York: Abbeville Press Publishers, 1999.

Day, Jeff and David Schiff, eds. *Walls, Walks, & Patios: Plan, Design, and Build.* Upper Saddle River, N.J.: Creative Home Owner Press, 1997.

Dennis, John V. *A Complete Guide to Bird Feeding.* New York: Alfred A. Knopf, Inc., 1975, 1994.

Erler, Catriona Tudor. *Garden Rooms.* Alexandria, Va.: Time-Life Books, 1999.

Familiar Butterflies: North America, The Audubon Society Pocket Guide. New York: Alfred A. Knopf, 1990.

Flexner, Bob. *Understanding Wood Finishing: How to Select and Apply the Right Finish.* Emmaus, Pa.: Rodale Press, Inc., 1994.

Freudenberger, Richard. *Building Fences + Gates: How to Design and Build Them from the Ground Up.* Asheville, N.C.: Lark Books, 1997.

Harrison, Kit and George Harrison. *America's Favorite Backyard Wildlife.* New York: Simon & Schuster, Inc., 1987.

Hayward, Gordon. *Garden Paths: A New Way to Solve Practical Problems in the Garden.* New York: Houghton Mifflin Co., 1998.

Heddy, Edward J. And Pete Peterson. *The Complete Guide to Decorative Landscaping with Brick and Masonry.* Crozet, Va: Betterway Publications, Inc., 1990.

Joyce, Ernest, with revisions and updating by Alan Peters. *Encyclopedia of Furniture Making.* New York: Sterling Publishing Co., Inc, 1987.

Knox, Gerald M. *Better Homes and Gardens® Complete Guide to Gardening.* Des Moines, Iowa: Better Homes and Gardens® Books, 1979.

Knox, Gerald M., ed. *Better Homes and Garden Step-by-Step Landscaping: Planning, Planting, Building.* Des Moines, Iowa: Meredith Corp., 1991.

Kramer, Jack. *Fences, Walls, and Hedges for Privacy and Security.* New York: Charles Scribner's Sons, 1975.

Loewer, Peter and Craig Tufts. *The National Wildlife Federation's Guide to Gardening for Wildlife: How to Create a Beautiful Backyard Habitat for Birds, Butterflies and Other Wildlife.* Emmaus, Pa.: Rodale Press, 1995.

Needham, Bobbe. *Beastly Abodes: Homes for Birds, Bats, Butterflies & Other Backyard Wildlife.* New York/Asheville, N.C.: Sterling/Lark Books, 1996.

Pavord, Anna. *The Border Book.* New York: Dorling Kindersley Publishing, Inc., 1994, 2000.

Proctor, Noble, Dr. *Garden Birds: How to Attract Birds to Your Garden.* Emmaus, Pa.: Rodale Press, 1986.

Reed, David. *The Art and Craft of Stonescaping: Setting and Stacking Stone.* Asheville, N.C.: Lark Books, 1998.

Sheldon, Kathy. *Designing and Planting Backyards.* Alexandria, Va.: Time-Life Books, 2000.

Stevens, David. *Garden Walls and Floors.* London: Conran Octopus Limited, 1999.

Swift, Penny and Janek Szymanowski. *Build Your Own Outdoor Structures in Brick.* London: New Holland (Publishers) Ltd., 1997.

———. *Build Your Own Walls and Fences.* London: New Holland (Publishers) Ltd., 1996.

Terrance Conran's Garden DIY. London: Conran Octopus Limited, 1995.

The editors of Time-Life Books. *Yard & Garden Projects: Easy, Step-by-Step Plans and Designs for Beautiful Outdoor Spaces.* Alexandria, Va.: Time-Life Books, 1998.

Whitner, Jan Kowalczewski. *Stonescaping: A Guide to Using Stone in Your Garden.* Pownal, Vt.: Storey Communications, Inc., 1992.

Wilkinson, Elizabeth. *The House of Boughs.* New York: Viking Penguin, Inc., 1985.

Index

Adirondack love seat project, 100–103
arbors, 67

Bases (path foundation)
    cement-pouring for, 24–25
    depth of, 22–23, 24
    drainage, 20
    drainpipes in, 23, 25–26
    edging shelves, 21, 23, 27
    for grass paths, 30–31
    hand-tamping soil in, 24
    preparation of, 20–26
    use of landscape cloth, 23–24
bats
    bat house project, 78–79
    habitat considerations, 74, 76
bays (fence), 52–54
birdbaths
    decorating project, 83–84
    winter protection of, 83
birds
    feeding, 80–81
    habitat considerations, 74–76
    plants for, 80
    shelter for, 82
    water for, 81–84
bleaching, of fences, 69
block walls, 62, 69
bond stones, 65
borders
    entryways for, 66–67
    height considerations, 45
    legal considerations, 45, 46, 60
    overview, 43
    safety, 44–45
    site enhancement, 44–45
    site plans for, 46–47
    weather, 44
border types
    fences, 52–59
    hedges, 48–51
    walls, 60–65
bricks
    dry-laying, 37
    how to cut, 113
    maintenance of, 38
    mortaring, 37–38
    overview, 17–18
    pattern tips, 37
    types of, 114
brick walls, 61, 69
building bricks, 114
butterflies
    butterfly box project, 88–89
    garden plan for, 86–87
    habitat considerations, 85
    life cycle of, 85
    roosts for, 74

Caps (wall), 65
cats
    fences for, 45
    wildlife and, 73
cement bases, pouring, 24–25
chair and table project, 104–9
children
    borders for, 45
    wildlife and, 72
common bricks, 114
concrete footings. *See* footings
concrete furniture, 95
concrete paths
    construction, 39–41
    design tips, 39, 40, 41
    maintenance, 41
    overview, 18–19
control joints, 41
courses (wall), 65
coyotes, 73
cross-slope grading
    base slope and, 23, 24
    for increasing slope, 21
crusher run gravel. *See* gravel (base)
cut stones
    design tips, 33–34
    dry-laying, 34
    maintenance of, 35
    mortaring, 34–35
    overview, 15–16
cutting
    bricks, 113
    stone, 111–12

Dadoes, 53
deck project, 98–99
decorated birdbath project, 83–84
decorative stones. *See* gravel (surface)
deer, 45, 77
depth, of bases, 22–23, 24
dogs
    fencing for, 45
    wildlife and, 73
drainage. *See also* drainpipes
    base construction and, 23–24
    flatness of path and, 21
    slopes and, 21
    testing soil for, 20
drainpipes, in bases, 23, 25–26
dry-laying
    cut stones, 34
    natural stones, 35–36
dry-stacked stone walls, 61

Edges (habitat), 75
edgings
    digging shelves for, 23
    gardens and, 32
    installation of, 27
    path layout and, 21
entryways, 66–67
expansion-joint strips, 39, 40–41

Face bricks, 114
fences
    bays, 52–54
    decorating, 68–69
    footings, 52–53, 57
    framework, 53–54
    infill choices, 54
    laying out lines for, 54–55
    picket fence project, 58–59
    postholes, 55–57
fieldstones. *See* natural stones
finishes, outdoor wood and, 115–16

INDEX

flagstones. *See* natural stones
flatness of path. *See* drainage
flowers, for butterfly garden, 86–87
flying squirrels, 76
footings
    for fences, 52–53, 57
    for walls, 62–63, 64, 65
form boards, 24–25
framework (fence), 53–54
freezing. *See* weather effects
furniture
    Adirondack love seat project, 100–103
    choosing locations for, 92–93
    functions of, 92
    made of concrete, 95
    made of metal, 94–95
    made of plastic resin, 94
    made of wicker, 93–94
    made of wood, 93
    portable deck project, 98–99
    secondhand, 95
    table and matching chair project, 104–9
    tips for building, 96
    tips for buying, 96

Garden plan for butterflies, 86–87
gates, 66–67
grading, cross-slope, 21
grass paths
    bordered by gardens, 32
    maintenance of, 32
    overview, 14–15
    sod installation, 31
    soil preparation, 30–31
    sowing *See*d for, 32
    species requirements, 15
gravel-and-earth footings, 52
gravel (base), 23–24
gravel (surface)
    adding, on top of bases, 28
    bare feet and, 10, 13
    importance of edging with, 28
    maintenance of, 29
    overview, 13

Habitats, 74–76
heat-zone map, 119
heaving. *See* weather effects
hedges
    contrasted with other borders, 44, 45
    laying out lines for, 54–55
    overview, 48
    planting project, 50–51
    plants for, 51
    pruning, 68
    selection considerations, 48–49, 51

Infill
    choices, 54
    pickets, 58–59
insects, 76

Landscape cloth, 23–24
laying out paths, 20–21
legal considerations
    and border heights, 45
    and borders, 46
    and hiring professional workers, 110
    and wall footings, 60
love seat project, 100–103
lumber sizes, 118

Maps, heat-zone, 119
metal furniture, 94–95
metric conversions, 118
mortared stone wall project, 64–65
mortaring
    cut stones, 34–35
    natural stones, 34–35, 36
    rendering, 69
mortises (through), 53
mosaic-decorated birdbath project, 83–84
mulches, for path surfaces, 12, 24, 28

Natural stones
    dry-laying, 35–36
    mortaring, 34–35, 36
    overview, 16–17
    pattern tips, 35, 36
noise, buffering, 45

Organic materials, for path surfaces, 12, 24, 28
ornamental stones. *See* gravel (surface)
outdoor furniture. *See* furniture
outdoor table and matching chair project, 104–9

Painting, on walls and fences, 69
paths. *See also* path surfaces; specific path surface materials
    building costs, 11
    edgings for, 27
    installing surfaces, 28–41
    laying out, 20–21
    overview of path surfaces, 12–19
    preparing bases for, 20–26
    site decisions, 10–11
    walking comfort and slope of, 21
path surfaces
    base depth requirements for, 24
    bricks, 17–18, 36–38
    concrete, 18–19, 39–41
    cut stones, 15–16, 32–35
    decorative stones, 13, 28–29
    grass, 14–15, 30–32
    gravel, 13, 28–29
    how to trim and cut stone for, 111–12
    mulches, 12, 28
    natural stones, 16–17, 35–36
    overbuying stone for, 110
    overview, 12–19
    stepping stones, 29–30
paver bricks, 114
paving materials. *See* path surfaces
picket fence project, 58–59
planning. *See* site planning
plans, butterfly garden, 86–87
planting a hedge project, 50–51
plants
    for butterfly garden, 86–87
    for decorating walls and fences, 68
    for hedges, 51
plastic resin furniture, 94
ponds, 75
portable deck project, 98–99

INDEX

postholes, 55–57
posts (fence), 53–54
privacy, borders for, 44
professional workers, hiring considerations, 110
projects
   building a bat house, 78–79
   building a butterfly box, 88–89
   building a mortared stone wall, 64–65
   building an Adirondack love seat, 100–103
   building a picket fence, 58–59
   building a portable deck, 98–99
   decorating a birdbath with mosaic, 83–84
   outdoor table and matching chair, 104–9
   planting a hedge, 50–51
pruning hedges, 68

Rabbits, 77
raccoons, 77
rails (fence), 53–54
rendering, 69
resin furniture, 94
road bond. *See* gravel (base)
rubble, 65

Secondhand outdoor furniture, 95
security
   borders and, 44–45
   entryways and, 67
seed preferences (bird), 81
shelves (edging), 21, 23, 27
site planning. *See also* wildlife
   birds, 80–82
   borders, 46–47
   butterflies, 85–87
   entryways, 66–67
   overview, 7
   paths, 9–19
   wildlife fencing, 45
slope (degree of incline)
   adjusting, of ground, 22
   calculating, 21–22

checking, while digging base, 23
slopes (inclined ground)
   building steps on, 26
   drainage and, 21
   walking comfort on, 21
sod, installation of, 31
squirrels (flying), 76
squirrels (tree), 76–77
stepping stones, 29–30
steps, on slopes, 26
stone. *See also* path surfaces; specific types of stones
   common types of, 113
   how to trim and cut, 111–12
   overbuying, 110
   wall project, 64–65
   walls, 61
surfaces. *See* path surfaces

Table and matching chair project, 104–9
tamping, base soil, 24
through mortises, 53
tree squirrels, 76–77
trimming stone, 111–12

Used outdoor furniture, 95

Veneers, for concrete-block walls, 69

Walking comfort
   on gravel, 10, 13
   slope of paths and, 21
walkways. *See* paths
walls
   of block, 62
   of brick, 61
   building a stone wall project, 64–65
   constructing footings for, 62–63
   decorating, 68–69
   determining footing dimensions, 62
   laying out lines for, 54–55
   overview, 60
   rendering, 69
   of stone (*see* stone)

weather effects
   on birdbaths, 83
   borders and, 44
   on brick, 17–18, 39
   on concrete, 18–19, 40–41
   on cut stone, 15–16
   fence footings and, 52
   on grass, 14, 15
   gravel and, 13
   on natural stone, 17
   on path materials, 10–11
weed control
   edging and, 27
   landscape cloth for, 23–24
white washing, of fences, 69
wicker furniture, 93–94
wildlife. *See also* individual creatures
   attracting, 74–76, 78–89
   children and, 72
   creating habitats for, 74–76, 78–89
   deterring, 45, 73, 76–77
   fencing for, 45
   household pets and, 45, 72–73
   neighbors and, 72
   overview, 71
wood
   as choice for outdoor furniture, 93
   finishing, for outdoor use, 115–16
   lumber sizes of, 118
   types of, for outdoor use, 117
wythes, 65

Zone map, 119